Conscience and Responsibility

ERIC MOUNT, JR.

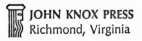 JOHN KNOX PRESS
Richmond, Virginia

Standard Book Number: 8042-0817-4
Library of Congress Catalog Card Number: 76-82937
© M. E. Bratcher 1969
Printed in the United States of America

To Truly, my beloved alter ego

Acknowledgments

Although this book's form bears little resemblance to the doctoral dissertation which was its ancestor, its conception and content are the fruits of the research which produced the dissertation of the same title which was completed at Duke University in 1966 under the direction of Professor Waldo Beach.

Professor Beach's helpful guidance aided and informed a systematic and sustained pursuit of interests which had been kindled earlier in the writer by Professors H. Richard Niebuhr and James Gustafson during a master's program at Yale Divinity School. It was Professor Niebuhr who first stimulated my interest in reflection on moral selfhood. It was Professor Gustafson whom I first heard express the need in Christian ethics for more work on the nature and function of conscience. My deep indebtedness to the teaching and writing of these three professors of Christian ethics will be easily apparent to readers either of the dissertation or of this book.

The actual preparation of this manuscript has been furthered by a research grant from Centre College, and by the typing of the two drafts by Mrs. Claudia Owens Robertson and by Mrs. Phyllis Emerson. My able co-worker Mrs. Ida Webster has assisted with a number of details and afforded protection that enabled the meeting of deadlines. Finally, my wife, Truly, has my deepest gratitude not as much because of her careful proofreading and apt suggestions as because she actually believed this book would be published, but still would have believed in me if it had not been.

Contents

The Context for
I a Contemporary Consideration
of Conscience

I go after reality with language. Perhaps I'd like to change it all into language, to force Madeleine and Gersbach to have a *conscience*. There's a word for you. I must be trying to keep tight the tension without which human beings can no longer be called human. If they don't suffer, they've gotten away from me.

. . . .

But let's stick to what matters. I really believe that brotherhood is what makes a man human. If I owe God a human life, this is where I fall down. "Man liveth not by Self alone but in his brother's face. . . . Each shall behold the Eternal Father and love and joy abound." When the preachers of dread tell you that others only distract you from metaphysical freedom, then you must turn away from them. The real and essential question is one of our employment by other human beings and their employment by us. Without this true employment you never dread death; you cultivate it. And consciousness when it doesn't clearly understand what to live for, what to die for, can only abuse and ridicule itself.[1]

But "the death of God," as a cultural fact of the modern age, is itself something whose fundamental cause, I believe, is to be sought in the "death of man" in our time, for this is the really primary fact in modern experience. What we confront, throughout the whole polity of modern society, is a tragic devitalization of the very concept of the person.[2]

A Persistent Concern

Herzog's wrestle with the meaning of true humanity in terms of conscience and living "in his brother's face" illustrates a struggle with which literature has perennially had to deal. Despite what Wylie Sypher calls the loss of the self in modern literature and art,[3] referring to the anonymous, "adjusted," socialized man, man's understanding of his moral selfhood is considered by more writers than Bellow today. The search for identity, which pervades much contemporary writing, is a clear indication that total "adjustment" is far from effected. We are not so sure what conscience is, and there is great confusion as to what authority conscience can or should own either for the atheist or the contemporary Catholic, Jew, or Protestant. Yet conscience and the meaning of moral selfhood are often as much a concern to contemporary writers as they were to John Bunyan or John Milton. Frank, the Assistant, in Bernard Malamud's book by that name is a conscience-stricken man. Gavin, the central character in Brian Moore's *Emperor of Ice Cream,* comes to the conclusion that there is no other sovereign of the self than the imaginary Emperor, but the story traces his maturing as a conscientious person. Two of the most talked-about plays in recent years have focused on churchmen caught in a crisis of conscience. In Rolf Hochhuth's *The Deputy,* the Pope's refusal to use the power of his office against Hitler is contrasted with the conscientious opposition of a priest named Riccardo Fontana and a Protestant in the German SS named Kurt Gerstein. Robert Bolt's *Man for All Seasons* finds its power in Thomas More's unerring faithfulness to his ultimate commitments, or, as one reviewer worded it, "his own fidelity to selfhood,"[4] even at the cost of his life. Perhaps the appeal of the play is in its contrast to the danger of the loss of selfhood Sypher expounds.

In areas of business and politics, there have been books for the conservative conscience by Senator Goldwater's ghost-writer and for the liberal conscience (Stewart Currie Brown's study of Adlai Stevenson entitled *Conscience in Politics*). In the 1964 election voters were asked to vote for Goldwater because they knew in their hearts he was right; and President Johnson has addressed more than one appeal to the heart and conscience of his fellow Americans. Former Secretary of Commerce, Luther Hodges, writes *The Business Conscience* and national magazines devote features to the responsible businessman. Martin Luther King saw the black man as the white man's conscience although the threatening chaos of today feeds on the disillusionment of his dream. Pope Paul urges his peace appeals on the conscience of all men of goodwill. The Vietnamese war has drawn frequent reference to a crisis of conscience[5] and occasioned a flurry of writing on selective conscientious objection.

The world come of age may not be religious, but it is still conscientious provided that adjective is not construed as referring to a certain way of life. We may be living in the midst of a value vacuum in a time of revolution that makes all authorities suspect, but there still seems to be an assumption about human responsibility which is very much alive in this era of secularization.

Equate conscience with the oppressive parental hangover of the superego, and the Freudians may grudgingly accept it as the necessary but suspect civilizer. Insist that it involves human freedom and responsibility, and the neo-behaviorists may discount it. Call it the stultifying vestige of our Puritan past, and Madison Avenue and Hugh Hefner will seduce it. Make it the independent mind, and totalitarians both foreign and home-grown will seek to ban it. Define it as the judgmentalism of the dogmatist, and the "tolerant" won't tolerate it. Equip it with rules, and the new moralists will liberate it. Reduce it to a heedless antinomianism, and the churches will dispute it. Attempt to give it content, and the sociologist will relativize it. Try to locate it, and the linguistic analysts will question it. Reduce it to man's accusor, and the Catholics will attack it; make it a human faculty or capability, and the Protestants will dispute it.

On every hand one finds definitional difficulties to the extent that such terms as *identity, integrity, responsibility,* and *obligation* are often preferred. Still, a look at the politics and prose of our time, even a look that allows for false piety at vote-polling time and for the quirks of the *literati,* prompts the conclusion that conscience as a term and as a reality is not dead, whatever fate may have been assigned to God. The old girl is asserted to be on her last legs by some who picture her in Victorian garb and identify her with societal stultification of the self, but she has started making appearances on the other side of the street under such sponsorship as the right of dissent and the importance of personal autonomy. And her new costumes reveal that she still has a good pair of legs. "Let your glands be your guide" has not carried the day as yet.

In addition to this popular persistence, conscience is making a comeback in Christian ethical thought. After a period of being relegated to a place of importance ranging from subordinate to negligible in Protestant thought, conscience has been receiving renewed attention. The revival of concern with moral selfhood in general has involved, in a number of notable instances (such as Dietrich Bonhoeffer, Gerhard Ebeling, Paul Lehmann, H. Richard Niebuhr, Helmut Thielicke, and Paul Tillich), a reassessment of the nature and function of conscience by prominent Protestant ethicists and the beginning of dialogue concerning the concept of conscience with Roman Catholic thinkers, in whose tradition *conscience* has generally remained an important term. The concept of conscience, which is coming to life in the thought of Christian ethicists who are genuinely contemporary, is not, however, a mere resuscitation of an older body of tradition. The Christian community is having to learn to cope with new problems, to recognize new conditions in its cultural setting, and to understand and relate to new developments in psychology, sociology, and philosophy if it expects anyone to listen when it uses the word *conscience*.

In its recovery of the concept of conscience, the Christian community is faced with numerous problems which did not confront the church in earlier periods when Western culture was as yet pre-scientific and not yet "post-Christian." While conscience is still part of popular parlance and often a subject of academic discussion, the various modern schools of thought in philosophy and social sciences have called traditional notions of conscience into question to such an extent as to render its meaning ambiguous and its usage problematic for many. While cultures in which Christianity has been influential still evidence at least a residue of what many would call "the Christian conscience," the source is often not acknowledged and the substance is more often than not either diluted or rejected. Neither the ambiguity of conscience nor the secularization of conscience is necessarily a curse. These are rather facts that may either plague the Christian community or prompt it to a recovery of conscience which neither succumbs to every wind of scientific and philosophical doctrine nor ignores these currents of secular thought.

The Secular Setting as Challenge

At the risk of gross oversimplification and the mating of bedfellows which would make even politicians blush, two general trends in thought which have influenced conceptions of conscience can be traced as aids to a grasp of the contemporary secular setting of our problem. One of these is subjectivist, autonomous, and individualistic in flavor; the other is objectivist, heteronomous, and collectivist in nature. The expressions of each are responses to the expressions of the other, and within each are expressions which may bear more similarity at points to representatives of the other trend than to some in its own group.

A modern survey of the subjective side could begin with the Renaissance and the Reformation. After Luther asserted the priority of his scripturally-informed conscience over the authority of Rome, the potentiality for believers with their Bibles to part company "conscientiously" with other believers (also with their Bibles) was greatly heightened. When René Descartes urged radical doubt about the individual mind's contact with "objective reality," he created a split from which Western philosophy has not yet recovered, and the effects of his epistemological uncertainties were soon to be felt in ethics. The Catholic ethicist Charles Curran has written with justification, "Ever since Descartes, philosophers like Montaigne, Rousseau and Kant have overemphasized the subjective element."[6] In the case of Kant, a feeling of oughtness was posited as being universal, but this imperative was reduced to a legalistic inner voice without the sanction of any external authority. Paul Lehmann has observed that Kant's interiorization of conscience resulted in a severing of the linkage between man's inner nature and the external ordering of life which Greek thought had posited and Christian theology had furthered in a transformed version.[7] Man's reaction against authoritarian tutelage and his outgrowing of unconsidered acquiescence were healthy, but there were accompanying dangers.

Like the first trend, the emphasis on objectification has its eminent representatives, its salutary contributions, and its reductionistic tendencies. One can see it as the creator as well as the destroyer of a true notion of conscience which Charles Curran subsumes under "over-objectification." Curran's objections to objectification aim at those who make conscience "merely a function of physiological factors (Chauchard), psychological factors (Freud) or sociological factors (Durkheim)."[8] The materialistic metaphysics of Thomas Hobbes had, as Tillich rehearses, made man a reaction to stimuli.[9] The utilitarian psychology of Jeremy Bentham made man a captive to pain and pleasure. Fellow utilitarian John Stuart Mill was optimistic about the harmonization of the inclination of the individual and the interests of society and presented a qualified heteronomy. Socialization via the child's moral training enabled the rational unification of inclination and obligation. In other words the pain and pleasure of others as well as his own becomes the interest of the self. By contrast, Darwin's evolutionary naturalism reduced conscience to the residue of a race's instinct for survival. Freud's psychoanalytic approach made conscience the unconscious repository for the influence and sanctions of authority figures. The essence of conscience becomes the dread of society. In the inner conflict between the instinctive drive for pleasure (id) and the reality of one's environment, the superego is the receiver which picks up the restrictions which parental or other authorities would impose. The superego may make positive and necessary contributions toward civilized living, but it is predominantly negative in its censoriousness.[10] Thus man is inhibited by this negative, repressive superego and needs release from the burden of his guilt.

Friedrich Nietzsche's view of conscience is an extremely heteronomous one which stands in dramatic contrast to the utterly autonomous style of life which he advocated. For him conscience was not even the necessary civilizer of the Freudian; it represents the sinister repression of society. True selfhood is found through the assertion of the individual's creative will in independence of all relationships to other selves. In Wylie Sypher's words, Nietzsche's rebellion against society's sanctions is so extreme that he is "an arch individualist in an age of individualism."[11] What he labels "conscience" is the bad conscience brought on by the self's acceptance of social strictures. This guilt is a sickness to be gotten over as man evolves to a nobility which is beyond good and evil. Conscience grows out of the necessary suppression of man's aggressive, destructive, willful instincts by rulers which results in the turning inward of these instincts in self-punishment.[12] Although he would never use the term *conscience*, Nietzsche is actually advocating his own brand of anarchically-autonomous conscientiousness in rebellion against heteronomous definitions of true selfhood. In less extreme forms later existentialists also assert autonomy without necessarily relegating the word *conscience* to the blacklist. Heidegger's contribution on this score is an example which is treated later.

The social psychology of George Herbert Mead is an example of an emphasis on the collective shaping of the individual which stands in sharp contrast to Nietzsche's jaundiced view of the internalization by the self of others' image of it. For Mead with his behavioristic starting point man experiences himself only indirectly and by way of the standpoints of individuals in his group or from the "generalized standpoint of the social group as a whole."[13] His point is that we know ourselves only through one another or "the generalized other" although we do not exist only in others' presence. To become a subject to oneself, one first becomes an object to himself just as others are to him, and he does this by assuming the attitude or attitudes of others toward him in his social environment. We shall have occasion to appropriate and also to take exception to Mead's contribution in elaborating a view of conscience which draws from Mead via H. Richard Niebuhr.

There have been notable contemporary attempts to counteract the heteronomous conscience and to recover an autonomous
understanding of conscience which does not locate it simply in
the reason or will or emotions.[14] Martin Heidegger's *Being and
Time* includes his existentialist effort as a reassessment of the
concept of conscience. The Freiburg philosopher describes conscience as the call of a being to itself, a summons to leave the
anonymity of "they-ness" for the authentic existence of personal
commitment in acceptance of "being toward death." Conscience, the call of care, is the demand to actualize one's potentialities, to accept responsibility towards oneself and accept
guilt, since existence as such is guilty and only self-deception
can preserve a good moral conscience.[15] Tillich writes in appraisal of Heidegger, *"The good, transmoral conscience consists in the acceptance of the bad, moral conscience,* which is
unavoidable whenever decisions are made and acts are per-
formed."[16] Bad conscience is to be lived with rather than outgrown as Nietzsche advocates.

In psychology some post-Freudian psychoanalytic theorists
have insisted on an autonomous ego rather than Freud's subservient ego, driven by the wishes of id and intimidated by the
tyrannical, forbidding secret policeman of the self, the superego.
As Lindzey and Hall explain it, "a new 'ego-psychology' has
been evolved, a psychology in which the ego is depicted as being
a rational institution responsible for intellectual and social
achievements and one whose functioning is not solely dependent upon the wishes of the id. It has its own sources of energy,
its own motives and interests, and its own objectives."[17]

Karen Horney, a Freudian revisionist, takes issue with
Freud's identification of superego as only a more exacting version of the normal phenomenon of conscience and ideals and
with his calling them both a discharge of cruelty against the
self. She insists on a clear distinction between the superego and
the ego-ideal.

> Leaving apart the philosophical intricacies involved in the
> definition of ideals, one may say that they represent the
> standard of feelings or behavior which the individual
> himself recognizes as valuable and obligatory to him.

They are not ego-alien but are an integral part of the self. To them the "super-ego" has but a superficial resemblance. It would not be quite correct to say that the content of the need to appear perfect coincides only incidentally with the culturally approved moral values: the perfectionistic aims would not fulfill their various functions if they did not coincide with the approved standards. But they only ape the gestures of moral norms.[18]

Also on the psychoanalytic side and related to Horney's bone of contention with Freud is Erich Fromm's distinction between authoritarian conscience (Freud's internalization of external authority) and humanistic conscience, "the reaction of our total personality to its proper functioning or dysfunctioning; not a reaction to the functioning of this or that capacity but to the totality of capacities which constitute our human and our individual existence."[19] The authoritarian superego is only a preliminary stage in the development of conscience. Its content comes from commands and taboos, not from one's own value judgments. Humanistic conscience is one's own voice calling the self to be responsible to itself in independence of external sanctions and rewards. Self-respect is substituted for social approval. "Humanistic conscience is the expression of man's self-interest and integrity, while authoritarian conscience is concerned with man's obedience, self-sacrifice, duty, or his 'social adjustment.' The goal of humanistic conscience is productiveness and, therefore, happiness, since happiness is the necessary concomitant of productive living."[20]

Heidegger is an existentialist representative, and Fromm is a psychoanalytic one of the widespread attempt to correct heteronomy or other-directedness or the psychology of adjustment by reversion to autonomy. Fromm realizes that a person derives his sense of selfhood from community involvement, but he could have been quoting Heidegger or Jean-Paul Sartre when he wrote these lines: "No power transcending man can make a moral claim upon him. Man is responsible to himself for gaining or losing his life. Only if he understands the voice of his conscience, can he return to himself."[21] As Roger Shinn insists, Fromm's man is not individualistic or even tribal man, but universal man. The rationally conscientious must create a communitarian society to replace the fallen system which enslaves perfectable and essentially unfallen man.[22] Despite the communal concern, however, Fromm's title *Man for Himself* and his description of the humanistic conscience has a decidedly autonomous, though not narrowly individualistic, slant.

Both autonomy and heteronomy, both subjectivist and objectivist emphases, both the stress on the individual and that on the collective influence make positive contributions to our understanding of conscience. The interesting thing is that the pendulum swings from autonomy to heteronomy without much allowance for theonomous possibilities. There seems to be a pervasive insistence that God not be invoked to explain conscience either as his voice or as a necessary presupposition for the sensitive and sound conscience. Fromm even contends that his own shedding of theology for psychological anthropology is a logical outgrowth of the Old Testament tradition.[23] The desire to separate God and conscience is easy to understand. When one contemplates the blunders wrought by the religiously conscientious, it is not hard to imagine that God enjoys more being invoked less. We did not need T. V. Smith's warning to fear "a little totalitarian operating in the bosom of every conscientious man, especially if he is a middle man operating in the name of God."[24] As Gerstein exclaims in *The Deputy:*

> Conscience? Who could trust that!
> Conscience or God:
> men never have wreaked such havoc
> as when invoking God—or an idea.[25]

Post-Christian profession has often been accompanied by a facsimile of Christian practice, but the Nazi conscience of Adolph Eichmann is grim evidence of what conscience can become when its authority is a madman who took Nietzsche's brand of irrational transmorality at face value. Hannah Arendt, in her account of the Eichmann trial,[26] reveals the scrupulosity of the Jew-slayer's conscience. Toward the end of the war, Eichmann's attitude and actions in relation to the Jews changed from an earlier stance which was humane by comparison with the later genocidal program. Although he had at first helped organize massive emigrations of Jews from Germany and the nations she occupied, when Hitler ordered his "Final Solution," extermination of the Jews, Eichmann adjusted his "conscience." In obedience to Hitler and in emulation of the zealous execution of the order by admired colleagues, Eichmann's conscience was converted. Miss Arendt writes, "He did not need to 'close his ears to the voice of his conscience,' as the judgment has it, not because he had none, but because his conscience spoke with a 'respectable' voice, with the voice of respectable society around him."[27] After his conversion, Eichmann was so conscientious that he felt guilty when he helped a half-Jewish cousin and a Jewish couple for whom his uncle pled. He even "confessed his sins," as he put it, to his superiors. Whereas conscience has traditionally been thought of as resister of murderous inclinations, Eichmann and his fellow Nazi killers have "learned how to resist the temptation" not to murder, as Arendt states.[28]

The Nazi conscience was an aberration, but it is one more contributor to the ambiguity the word carries with it for many today, an ambiguity to which Freud referred when he said in his thirty-first lecture on psychoanalysis:

> The philosopher Kant once declared that nothing proved to him the greatness of God more convincingly than the starry heavens and the moral conscience within us. The stars are unquestionably superb, but where conscience is concerned, God has been guilty of an uneven and careless piece of work, for a great many men have only a limited share of it or scarcely enough to be worth mentioning.[29]

This ambiguity has been reflected in the continuing confusion and disagreement with regard to conscience in philosophical circles which Bernard Wand tersely documents in his article "The Content and Function of Conscience":

> It has been said of conscience that it is fallible (Broad), that it is infallible (Butler); that its ultimate basis is emotional (Mill), that its ultimate source is rational (Rashdall); that it is the voice of God (Hartmann), or the voice of custom (Paulsen); that it is merely advisory (Nowell-Smith), . . . that it is conscious (Butler), that it is unconscious (Freud); that it is a faculty (Butler), that it is not (any contemporary moral philosopher); that it is the dis-

position to have certain beliefs, emotions, and conations which, when operative, issue in conscientious actions (Broad), and that it *is* conscientious action (Ryle).[30]

It is no wonder, in view of such discrepancies, that the confusion which the secularization of conscience has created for the church has been matched by a widespread suspicion of any usage of the term in many secular disciplines.

Theological Trends in Response

There are several ways in which the Christian community can react to what Paul Lehmann calls "the decline and fall of conscience."[31] The representatives of secularization and the contributors to confusion can be damned from a distance as instruments of the devil. They may be ignored by a sheltered ingroup which only talks to itself in supposed security from alien influences. Still another possibility is hearing them without capitulating to them. If this latter possibility is to become a reality, theologians must give evidence of their awareness of and appreciation for certain crucial areas of contemporary thought outside the bounds of theology. On the other hand they must avoid being adopters without adaptation of one of the current secular theories of conscience. One of the evidences of the dialogue with secular thought on the part of such thinkers as Bonhoeffer, Ebeling, Lehmann, and Niebuhr is the prominence they all give to the word *responsibility*, which has come into the linguistic currency of theology via psychology, sociology, existentialist philosophy, and other extra-theological disciplines.

There is, however, another reason why *responsibility* has assumed a place of prominence in the parlance of contemporary Christian ethics besides its extra-theological importance. Because it can have both inner and outer references, this term reflects the recognition of the inseparability of the self and society which is essential to both foci of current Christian ethical thought. Since a consideration of the self and its societies together is necessary if conscience is to be delivered both from autonomy and heteronomy, both from individualism and authoritarianism, conscience is increasingly being considered together with responsibility. Much of the frontier work in moral selfhood is being done by men who are relating these terms suggestively. This is not to say that responsibility is a good word which can be substituted for conscience or clear up all its ambiguity. In fact in some student circles today one can virtually get hissed at if he uses the term *responsibility* because it is so laden with the definitions those in authority seem to give it. If the word is used at all, it is construed more in terms of responsiveness than in connection with accountability of any kind. One of the things this student mood should impress upon us is that saying a person is or should be responsible tells us nothing until it is indicated in relation to whom one is to be responsible. This same point needs making about being conscientious.

The twin current concerns of Christian ethicists with the self and with society represent a synthesis of foci of the two eras which preceded this one. Following the prevailing individualism of the eighteenth and early nineteenth centuries, there came a preoccupation with social problems which was dominant by the end of the nineteenth century. Christian ethics had entered a period when issues of capitalism and socialism, war and peace, ameliorative legislation and social reform held the attention of the moralists. Man was viewed less individualistically and more as part of his economic, political, and social contexts. The focus was more on the institutions and communities which shaped him than on the dimensions of moral selfhood, or the virtues that characterized the responsible Christian. Salvation was largely viewed as social and this-worldly, and individual, other-worldly salvation seemed less important. The kingdom of God became a societal goal as well as a personal allegiance. Sin was interpreted more as a social disorder than as selfish depravity, although the latter emphasis was not forgotten. In the heyday of the Social Gospel, concern with problems of "character" was suspect and suggestive of pietism, individualism, and social irrelevance. Not until the optimism of the liberal hope was dashed on the rocks of two world wars did this trend lose its momentum.

Out of the theological neoorthodoxy which arose from the

wreckage of the dashed liberal hopes and out of the reconstructed neo-liberalism which emerged altered by the impact
of Barthianism has come a combination of two concerns or
trends. In the words of Waldo Beach, "The one movement is
psychological and inward, the other is sociological and out-
ward."[32] One focuses on the dynamics of moral selfhood, the
other on the dilemmas and strategy of social action and policy-
making. Often the trends are advanced by different thinkers.
H. Richard Niebuhr, for instance, concentrated his efforts
much more on the theology and psychology of Christian ethics
than on specific political and economic questions. John Bennett, by contrast, has centered his attention on questions of
church-state relations, war and peace, and the Christian's involvement in political and economic and racial problems. In
both Niebuhr and Bennett, however, there are contributions to
the other pole and appreciation of the insights of those on the
other side. Niebuhr's concern is always with the self in his various communities, and Bennett's orientation presupposes certain understandings of human selfhood in sin and salvation
which distinguish him from the liberalism of a day which has
passed. In some instances, both trends in Christian ethics have
received significant attention in the same men. Although Reinhold Niebuhr has never attempted to be a theologian in the
sense that his brother was, he has furnished us with a modern
masterpiece on Christian anthropology, *The Nature and Destiny of Man*,[33] as well as provided a continuing stream of political analysis and social commentary in such journals as *Christianity and Crisis*, which he fathered. His dual interests are expressed in one of his more recent titles, *The Self and the Dramas
of History*.[34]

The Direction of This Study

Almost all Christian ethicists today largely realize the impossibility of separating the self and its communities. When the
spotlight is on the moral agent, the culture of the self cannot be
left in darkness. When issues of civil rights and international

relations are the focal concern, these cannot be considered in isolation from an understanding of the structures of prejudice and the way man's immorality takes peculiar forms in his immoral societies. Whether the focus is inner or outer, the concerns must always be inclusive rather than exclusive. A renewed concern with conscience has had to reflect this realization. Conscience cannot be legitimately reduced either to an inner or an outer matter, either to social pressure or to a solitary sense. Neither individual independence or social engineering holds the key to understanding the Christian moral agent. The self and his societies must be considered together.

The twin considerations which will be pressed in the pages that follow afford a needed corrective to some of the oversimplifications which plague the popular "new morality" debate. It is sometimes implied that we must choose between standard and situation, between law and liberty. Morality consists, one might surmise, either in the application of moral universal principles to specific cases of conscience or in doing the loving act of the situation. The importance of principles or of the demands of the situation cannot be denied. But understanding of Christian moral selfhood and appreciation for the interwovenness of the self and its communities as continuing contexts of interaction are equally important and widely neglected. It is because of their attention to just those crucial concerns that the writer will be heavily indebted to H. Richard Niebuhr and James Gustafson in the analysis of conscience and responsibility which follows.

2 Barriers and Gateways to a Definition of Conscience

You cannot contemplate the individual man out of Society: you will scarcely find him among savages if you look diligently for him. But you must vindicate his position in order that you may show what Society is; of what it consists. If it does not consist of I's, of Persons, the Moralist has no concern with it. If it does consist of I's, of Persons, begin with asserting that character for it, then go on to investigate the relations in which the members of it stand to each other. That means, as I conceive, when translated into the book speech, "Begin with Casuistry [by which Maurice means the study of cases of conscience, not the dissemination of prescriptions or rules]; go on to Moral Philosophy. First make it clear what you mean by a Person; that you will do when you make it clear what you mean by a Conscience; then treat these Persons as if they did form real bodies, and tell us out of history, not out of your own fancy, what these bodies are."

Hereafter then, in any Course I may deliver upon Ethics; I shall be in the strictest sense occupied with Society; but with Society, as consisting of Persons; with Society, as implying the existence of a Conscience; strong in proportion as that is strong, weak as it is weak.[1]

F. D. Maurice gets to the heart of the matter when he makes the understanding of the meaning of *person* inseparable from the meaning of *conscience*. It is precisely such a connection which we shall hope to establish in this chapter and the next one as we assess both helps and hindrances to a more inclusive view of conscience and then attempt to state a working definition. The reader should not wait with bated breath for the definition of conscience to be delivered once and for all in the ensuing paragraphs. The multiplicity of understandings of the term which persists among us will not be eliminated here or anywhere else. However, it is essential that the freight the term will carry in this book now be unpacked, and Maurice's insight about the inseparability of one's view of personhood from one's view of conscience has crucial importance at this point. Helmut Thielicke, the continental Lutheran ethicist, has aptly elaborated this connection:

> The differences in the understanding of conscience clearly arise out of differences in the understanding of man. My view of conscience is determined by my understanding of what is the normative factor determining human existence, e.g., practical reason, utility, or the sociological or biological structure. Conscience is always incorporated within the framework of a particular anthropology. Hence it is always indicative of a specific self-understanding of human existence. To this degree the ambiguity of the concept is in fact a sign that the unifying center has been lost, and that there is now a wild and panic-stricken search for substitutes.[2]

An Approach to the Problem

The approach taken here to the nature and function of conscience and its relation to responsibility is that which H. Richard Niebuhr presents in his classic, *Christ and Culture,* under the heading "Christ the Transformer of Culture."[3] The question of how Christian theology and ethics relate to the intellectual achievements and the political and economic life of a society has received various answers. Some place the cultural contributions and concepts, for instance the philosophical expressions, of an era in opposition to the Christian message. There are perennial representatives of Tertullian's insistence that Jerusalem (theology) has nothing to do with Athens (philosophy). Another posture makes a rather easy harmony or identification between the highest human achievements of a culture and Christian truth. Walter Rauschenbusch could thus speak of the "democratization of God." A third way to relate Christ and culture is by way of a synthesis. Theology becomes the capstone or completion of philosophy. It makes a needed addition without contradicting. The medieval synthesis expressed in the Thomistic wedding of Aristotle and the Bible is exhibit A. Still another approach is the dualistic arrangement which faces the need to relate Christ and culture, theology and philosophy, the Sermon on the Mount and the state of the union, but stresses the irresolvable and uneasy tension between the two. Some Lutheran thought provides an example of this emphasis on paradox. The final stance, and the one we are adopting, is that which appreciates and appropriates the contributions of culture without swallowing them whole. Theology happily acknowledges indebtedness to philosophy but is careful to see that no one philosophical system becomes a straitjacket for the Christian gospel. Conversion occurs. In terms of our study, this means that the insights of psychology, philosophy, and other secular disciplines are welcomed but not baptized uncritically. Our approach then will be the welding of secular insights concerning personhood in general and conscience in particular, as transformed by the revelation of God in Jesus Christ, to contemporary theological insights.

In Paul we have a model of this conversionist approach with respect to conscience. As C. A. Pierce points out in his study *Conscience in the New Testament*,[4] Paul appropriated the Greek word for conscience (*syneidesis*) which was part of the common linguistic currency of the Hellenistic environment in which he sought to communicate the gospel. However, Paul Lehmann rightly takes issue with Pierce's claim that Paul's usage of *conscience* was not colored by Hebraic experience and perspective. Lehmann suggests that Paul's initial use of the term in his defense of his apostleship to the Corinthians (I Cor. 4:4) hints at a transformation of meaning from "an internal human faculty of judgment which functions to condemn"[5] to the meaning conveyed by *heart* in the Hebrew tradition. It is God, not conscience, which judges in Paul. In Romans 13:5 conscience is juxtaposed with wrath, implying the Hebraic view of response to God's ordering of the world. The context of conscience, now God's action, is thus transformed and so is the meaning of the word. Wrath is the result of man's disregard of limits set in the goodness of God the creator and redeemer for man's welfare. With wrath comes personal disintegration; whereas, by contrast, free obedience to the order of humanization preserves the integrity of the self. Wrath and conscience warn of dehumanization but do not effect humanization. Similar understandings are evident in Romans 9:1, where conscience is connected with Christ and the Holy Spirit, and Romans 2:15, where Paul speaks of a "law written on the heart."

In answering the question regarding meat offered to idols (I Cor. 8:7-13), Paul demonstrates what Lehmann calls "the contextual," rather than legalistic, reality of Christian conscience, and he also repudiates, with equal decisiveness, ethical anarchy. He does appropriate *conscience* for Christian ethics, but he indicates that it is useless unless it is theonomously conceived and thus transformed. Such a conception is described by Lehmann in interpretation of Paul:

> The *theonomous* conscience is the conscience immediately sensitive to the freedom of God to do in the always changing human situation what the humanizing aims and purposes require. The *theonomous* conscience is governed and directed by the freedom of God alone. Ultimately, it is in this freedom that the decisions of man are set, and from this freedom come the power and the transforming possibilities which give ethical shape to behavior.[6]

As faith seeks to understand itself using this approach, it appropriates rather than rejects the language and wisdom of the setting in which it must articulate itself. Not staying only within biblical categories or making revelation contradict all of man's knowledge, this stance looks to analyses of human selfhood in philosophy and the social sciences for raw materials for Christian anthropology and ethics. As F. D. Maurice expressed it, "We ought not to overlook any theory about Society which has any considerable influence on any considerable number of men."[7] Thus Mead, Freud, Heidegger, and Fromm should be heard and appreciated by the Christian who would understand moral selfhood.

However, care must always be exercised lest social psychology or existentialist philosophy become a straitjacket which confines the gospel instead of a malleable medium for understanding and communication of the gospel. From this viewpoint the efforts outside of theology by man to understand himself are neither to be ignored nor to be baptized. They are neither to be rejected without a sympathetic hearing nor appropriated without critical evaluation and faithful transformation. The task, as we see it, is not necessarily to discover what *conscience* meant for the New Testament writers, though that information is significant, but more important to see current concepts of conscience in light of the revelation in Jesus Christ of whom God is and of whom man is. Anthropology is neither totally derived from Christology as is the case in Karl Barth *(Christ and Adam)*[8] or Paul Lehmann, nor is it unreconstructed by Christology, a danger to which Bultmann and Tillich and much Roman Catholic moral theology have been known to succumb. In the first instance some secular anthropology invariably gets into the act in disguise, and in the second the gospel is either forced into a Procrustean bed or constitutes a helpful addition instead of effecting a radical renovation. It is on the first count for instance that Paul Ramsey questions whether Paul Lehmann really escapes secular theories of contextualism and Freudian philosophies of self-realization despite his protestations to the contrary. He charges, "Until an ethic in a Christian context is articulated more reflectively, the language of secular contextualism will tend to fill the vacuum left by—indeed exhibited by—repeated inarticulate reference to what God is doing in the world to keep human life human."[9] More than one starting point is necessary, but Christ must control Adam.

Definitions Which Confine and Confuse

It is always easier to say what you do not mean and to "knock" that with which you do not agree than to give others something of yours at which to shoot. Still there are certain definitions of conscience in relation to personhood which confine conscience or confuse this relationship objectionably. At least for our purposes, certain understandings of conscience need to be ruled out without suggesting that the word *conscience* cannot be used legitimately in ways other than this study will recommend.

One reductionism which has been perpetrated in various forms through the years is what we could call "the faculty fallacy." Even Bernhard Häring, whose discussion of conscience in his multivolume work, *The Law of Christ*, is a valuable landmark in contemporary Roman Catholic moral theology, reverts to referring to conscience as "the moral faculty." The impression is thus given that conscience is a part of the self rather than the function or expression of the total self. There have been those who have wanted to locate conscience in man's rational "faculty," such as Thomas Aquinas. In fairness to St. Thomas, we should hear Häring's contention that the Angelic Doctor did not in fact pit the intellect against the will and meant by "practical reason" what we might call "potential love."[10] Because Protestants are inclined to identify reason in Roman Catholic thought with the *ratio* of the Enlightenment, John Thomas's paper from the *Ecumenical Dialogue at Harvard* is instructive. He insists that what the Thomist means by *reason* is "man's power to grasp reality," which he is enabled to do by faith in the revelation of God as well as by natural cognition.[11] Even with these cautions, Häring would be the first to recognize that the Roman tradition has tended to fragment the self and to put undue faith in the health of man's reason even in his sinful state. Luther's designation of reason as a whore may need qualification, but there are ample evidences that she can be bought. In the words of Salvador de Madariaga in his book *Don Quixote*, ". . . the mind acts before the courts of conscience as a council for desire, and the cleverer the council the more likely the victory of the party."[12]

There are not only rationalistic reductionisms, of course, as seen in Kant and Thomas Aquinas; there are voluntaristic and emotive ones. Although the problems with each differ, the issue is the same as regards the faculty fallacy. The self needs to be seen as a totality. Conscience is not a part of the self, but a mode of its existence. We shall have occasion to tie our understanding of conscience to a duality in the self, but with H. Richard Niebuhr we object to the location of this duality by splitting the self into higher and lower parts. The inner conflict which is found in the self has often been confused by idealists such as

Kant and by Roman Catholic thinkers with the so-called "reason-passion" conflict and by such empiricists as Westermarck with a reason-emotion duality.[13]

A long-popular view of conscience held that it is a repository for innate moral knowledge, but the holders of such a view are a vanishing breed. The moral self does know its commitments and "have its principles," but the content of conscience is incidental to its commitments and loyalties, and its affording any particular code of conduct is potential rather than probable. There is, however, another attempt to preserve the good name of conscience amid the welter of human error which is very much alive and which has its problems. This "infallibility fallacy" needs examination.

Roman Catholic thought in particular with its natural law stress has underlined man's knowledge of and disposition toward the good (*synteresis*) which he must prudently implement in particular instances (*conscientia*). The imperative of *synteresis* remains infallible, but specific decisions may be errors of conscience. However, according to Father Häring, "Viewed correctly, the culpably erroneous judgment is not really a verdict of conscience at all."[14] With this faculty notion of conscience as providing an indelible disposition toward the good, one's conscientious action may not really be conscientious. This is tricky business. If it is not right conscience, it seems, it is not conscience. Eichmann then, to revert to an earlier illustration, could not have been acting conscientiously. Our contention is that one can be acting dreadfully and acting according to conscience.

The problems involved with viewing conscience as the angelic witness or impetus within, which the "conscientious" obey and the culpably evil reject, are multiplied by the "will-o'-the-wisp" character of the content of the devoted conscience. F. W. Boreham illustrates this illusory character of conscience in his book *The Uttermost Star*:

> The men who burned the martyrs were often as conscientious as the martyrs whom they burned. When, on the first of July, 1416, John Huss was bound to the stake, a poor

old peasant woman came to the place of execution bringing with her a faggot. She begged that it might be added to the pile round the stake. But when it was flung on, she was not content. It must, she said, be close up to the victim, so that it might help to consume him.

"Have I ever harmed you or yours," asked Huss, "that you are so bitter against me?"

"Never," was the reply; "but you are a heretic. Wood is scarce this year, and the winter, they say, is like to be a hard one. I can ill afford the faggot, but I would fain do God service by helping to rid the earth of an accursed heretic; and therefore I make the sacrifice."

"O holy simplicity!" exclaimed the martyr. And, reaching out his hand, he drew the faggot toward him, and placed it against his side. "Perhaps," he said, "the faggot may be a means of grace to both of us!"

"Give your body to be burned!" said Conscience to John Huss. "Give your faggot to burn him!" said Conscience to the peasant woman.

Is not this the Will-o'-the-Wisp?[15]

A view of conscience which is much discussed among philosophers of mind affords us another questionable definition. We shall call it the "principle-only fallacy." Gilbert Ryle's claim that conscience is the witness to moral principle in a decision-making situation means that for him it is only one of the competitors in moral conflict and is silent apart from conflict.[16] This drastically limits its scope or authority, for as Bernard Wand rejoins, "What makes conscience authoritative is not . . . its operativeness, but rather that it constitutes the final or conclusive reason a person can give for performing an action."[17] Ryle is, it seems, in the same boat (or raft?) with Huck Finn. Huck's "conscience" troubled him terribly because of his involvement in the escape of Jim, the slave, and his lying to Mr. Parker about whether he had seen any runaway slaves. He could not rest or sit still. He was convinced that he had "done wrong," but he also could not bring himself to turn Jim over to Parker. He says, "Then I thought a minute, and says to myself, hold on; s'pose you'd 'a' done right and give Jim up would you felt better than what you do now? No, says I, I'd feel bad—I'd feel just the same way I do now."[18] His "principles" told him to tell the truth and turn in "runaway niggers" but his loyalty to a friend opposed the dictates of his society. For this man's money, he acted on Jim's behalf out of conscience even though Huck felt he was going against conscience.

To the "principle-only fallacy" must now be added the "accuser-only fallacy." To the Roman Catholic, Protestant notions of conscience have often made it the accuser of man or his rationalizer to keep from admitting guilt, and this criticism of Protestant negativism is well-founded. A persistent strain in Lutheran thought, for instance, reflects only the negative side of the Reformer's ambivalent assessment of conscience. Häring makes this same point with regard to Calvinism, which he claims knows only an evil conscience due to its false notion of total depravity.[19] The upshot is that conscience is often viewed positively only in its absence, and the Christian's joy is in being freed from conscience which is linked with man's attempts to justify himself before God, to achieve a good conscience rather than know the comforted conscience of faith. Both Helmut Thielicke and Dietrich Bonhoeffer tend to fall prey to this one-sided negativism. Because of conscience's judgmental function and self-image-centered orientation in his view, Bonhoeffer agrees with Goethe that the man of action is without conscience.[20] As he sees it, responsibility acts; conscience only judges. Conscience keeps score. You cannot play the game and keep score at once, he is insisting.

Conscience most assuredly involves pangs of guilt after the act is a fact. It is a warning buzzer of the boundaries beyond which we cannot go and live with ourselves. It is the troubler of the self in its transgressions of the self's standards. It is more, however, than the guage of guilt or goodness with respect to a particular act. Such a limitation would make conscience an alarm bell which sounds only when provoked and satisfies only when silent. As Joseph Fletcher cautions, though with questionable support from the source he cites, conscience should include the direction as well as the review of action.[21] The Thomistic tradition's emphasis on conscience as maker of moral judgments provides a needed balance on this score.

Still another partially valid but woefully incomplete version of conscience is "the secret police slant." Its designation as the internalization of societal censorship recalls Freud's superego and is reiterated in such semi-serious definitions as H. L. Mencken's reference to "an inner voice that warns us somebody is looking" or Harry Ruby's equation of conscience with "a fear of being found out."[22] Reinhold Niebuhr raises objection to this reductionism: "The 'superego' is therefore no more than the pressure of society upon 'the ego' and it does not occur to Freud that the self has both the power to defy the community for the sake of its interests and for the sake of interests more inclusive than that of a given community."[23] The self has social as well as selfish impulses, and his conscience is not wholly determined by the pressures of any one of his societies or even of all his societies combined. His own desires and needs interact in dynamic reciprocity with the society's customs, but these very needs and desires are not developed and experienced in a social vacuum even when they transcend the interests of one's communities. Even societies can transcend themselves.

A full-blown understanding of conscience must encompass both the authoritarian conscience and the humanistic conscience (Erich Fromm), both the superego and the ego-ideal. Gordon Allport makes a parallel distinction in his book, *Becoming,* between the "must" and the "ought." "Must" is conscience as "the interiorized voice of the herd," evoking fear as motivation for conformity. It is, for Allport, a necessary first stage in the process of becoming. "Ought," or the generic conscience, designates appropriate or fitting decisions or actions in correspondence with one's own ideal self-image. External sanctions give way to internal; prohibition, fear, and "must" give way to preference, self-respect, and "ought"; habits of obedience give way to generic self-guidance. Unlike Fromm, Allport exalts the mature religious conscience, which would be increasingly "ought"-directed rather than "must"-directed. Fear of divine punishment is the rule of childish conscience, not of religious maturity. Peter Bertocci makes the sense of moral obligation a capacity independent of coercions of parent or tribe

because it is so different from childhood "musts."[24] While Allport agrees that there is a difference between "ought" and
"must," he deems "must" a primitive stage in growth toward
"ought." For him and for this writer, moral obligation is not
independent or innate as Bertocci suggests, but emergent.

A literary depiction of this shift from "must" to "ought" is
found in Brian Moore's *The Emperor of Ice-Cream*. Early in
the book, Gavin, the Irish youth who becomes a man in the
midst of his work with the wounded and dead during the bomb-
ing of Belfast in World War II, imagines angels sitting on his
shoulders during his inner struggles. On one shoulder sits his
White Angel, who counsels purity, diligence, and all the expectations of his Catholic rearing. On the other sits his Black Angel
advocating lecherous, blasphemous, and rebellious courses of
action. At the end of the story he hears a new, cold, grown-up
voice within him. Moore writes, "He heeded that voice, heeded
it as he had never heeded the childish voices of his angels. Black
Angel, White Angel: they had gone forever. His father was
crying. The voice would tell him what to do. From now on, he
would know these things."[25] We might question whether his
change could be that complete, whether the angels were gone
forever, but Gavin's experience illustrates well the movement
from "must" to "ought." What someone has called "the still
small voice that makes you feel still smaller"[26] was not an alien
voice but his own. It was not just his own, as we shall want
to say shortly, but it was his own. The authoritarian conscience
of the child is not to be equated with the mature, considered
internalizing of moral obligations. The latter represents not an
outgrowing of conscience but a growing up of conscience.

The need to include both superego and ego-ideal, to encompass both "must" and "ought," in an understanding of
conscience can also be approached in terms of guilt and shame.
James Lapsley in his "A Psycho-Theological Appraisal of the
New Left" indicates that "the shame dynamic" has emerged as
the primary determinant of cultural sanctions and individual
life style in contrast to an earlier "guilt dynamic." He writes,
"To rebel, one must fear the *shame* of not being a fully par-
ticipating human being more than the *guilt* of destroying the

persons and structures which prevent this."[27] Drawing on Gerhart Piers' connection of shame to a tension between the ego
and the ego-ideal and of guilt with conflicts between the ego and
the superego,[28] Lapsley relates shame to failure or falling short
and guilt to transgressing a code which may be unwritten and
even unconscious. Lapsley rightly avoids claiming that these
feelings can always be separated in making these distinctions,
but he makes an assertion about shame which is especially significant in view of the emphasis on social selfhood which will
be developed in this book. Citing Helen Merrill Lynd's *On
Shame and the Search for Identity*,[29] he suggests that whereas
guilt may not be relational, shame always is and that shame
has older roots in the self's development, probably going back
to the original separation anxiety. As Lapsley concludes,
"Shame is more directly linked with mother relationship and
guilt with father relationship, though this is far from an absolute distinction."[30]

A final reductionism to which exception needs to be taken
is the "function fallacy." Conscience does include a *moral function* in choices between right and wrong, but it refers even more
basically to the *transmoral fulcrum* of responsibility, to pair
terms from Tillich and Lehmann in their treatments of conscience.[31] Lehmann writes in his *Ethics in a Christian Context,*
"The fulcrum of human responsiveness is the conscience—that
delicate conjunction of the inner springs of human motivation
and of human judgment informed by the divine activity in a
single, decisive, and free act of obedience."[32] The Union professor is speaking here of the conscience of the Christian, but
his assertion concerning the fulcrum of human responsiveness
is generally applicable. Although his calling "conscience an *act*
of knowing and doing"[33] raises some questions itself, he is
rightly insisting that conscience has basically to do with man's
total selfhood as moral agent, assuming that a faith is basic for
morality. A loyalty to some center of value informs ethical decision and action.

One expression of the position which needs qualification
is found in Joseph Fletcher's *Situation Ethics*. In his eagerness
to combat the "faculty fallacy" we have mentioned, he posits

that conscience should be understood as a verb and not as a noun. "There *is* no conscience; 'conscience' is merely a word for our attempts to make decisions creatively, constructively, fittingly."[34] The choices Fletcher offers us are too few. While appreciating the concern that prompts the Cambridge Situationist's verbal tendencies at this point, one could hazard the reminder that we are concerned here as much about the self that decides and acts as we are about the decisions and actions of the self. Why not call conscience a pronoun, the I, the person? Man does not have a conscience. In this we join Fletcher. He is a conscience. Gerhard Ebeling expressed it well when he wrote, "Conscience is a matter of coming to expression of man himself."[35] The specific decisions of the self like the sense of guilt one's commitments may occasion are more the consequences than the core of conscience. Eleanor Humes Haney makes the same point when she writes, "It is not one faculty or act of the self but a way of the self's being and acting; it cannot be separated from the self who is being conscientious."[36]

Still another way of stating the correction we are suggesting is found in Stuart Hampshire's study of intentionality, *Thought and Action*. He writes, "In conduct a man needs a certain consistency, a sense of policy and direction, that relates one action to another in a form of life, in order that he should not be always undoing what he has previously done . . . If it is not obvious to him that what he is inclined to do is a part of one single, right policy and way of life, he will want to ask himself whether this action could not be seen as part of an altogether different, and unintended, policy or way of life, when it is added to his own past conduct."[37] Conscience then has to do with the self's established policies. *Character* is the traditional word for this chain of consistency.

Resources for a Reassessment of Conscience

Having questioned the adequacy of some understandings of conscience, we turn to an appraisal of resources which make a contribution to a reassessment of conscience. The search for such helps will not be limited to treatments of *conscience* by name since we have already indicated that the concern here is with the moral self in more inclusive terms than conceptions of conscience often encompass. We shall want to consider the insights forthcoming from certain ancient and current treatments of terms such as *heart, integrity,* and *responsibility.* More than that we shall have to think of views of man in general, for, as has been indicated, one's view of conscience goes along with his perspective on man.

Bernhard Häring's reference to "pure conscience" in I Timothy 1:5 under his section on "The 'Heart' in Scripture and Tradition"[38] and his designation of love as the animator and shaper of conscience as well as the essence of the "Christian morality of the heart,"[39] are but two indications of the consideration he is giving to the biblical understanding of heart as he analyzes the moral self. On the Protestant side of the discussion, Paul Lehmann relies heavily on the Hebraic view of heart in his reassessment of conscience. Conscience by name is conspicuous for its absence in the Old Testament; heart (lēb) is plentifully present. Lehmann draws an important distinction between the Greek understanding of conscience and the Hebrew conception of heart. Conscience meant cognitive self-knowledge which condemns the self for nonconformity with an external order. Heart, by contrast, connotes "the fundamental 'bond betwixt two' by means of which the 'knowledge of good and evil' shapes behavior."[40] Heart includes the cognitive, but it is not only intellectual in its knowing. The total self is involved in the thinking and knowing.[41] The heart's knowledge is relational. It responds to God's claim. The knowledge of the Greek conscience is basically conceptual; that of the Hebrew heart is covenantal. What the Greek conscience knows always accuses; what the Hebrew heart knows may indicate either harmony or disharmony in a relation. Lehmann gives this definition of heart:

> Thus the heart is the pivotal personal center of man's total response to the dynamics, direction and personal thrust of the divine claim upon him. In short, according to the

Old Testament, the heart—not the conscience—is the focus of responsible behavior and the fulcrum of man's humanity.[42]

The Gospels duplicate the Old Testament's silence about conscience and its emphasis on heart, and we have already seconded Lehmann's exposition of Paul's transformation of the Greek *conscience* through the influence of *heart*.

Lehmann is hard put to find recognition of the revolution Paul ignited until he gets to Luther and Calvin, and even these Reformers were "too preoccupied with the pretensions and anarchies of human sinfulness and too at home in the humanistic tradition to perceive the full revolutionary impact of the Pauline revolution upon the subjugation of the conscience in these traditions to the tight alliance between divine wrath and human guilt."[43] The revolution remains to be completed, but the ammunition is there for it in Luther and Calvin. Both of them perceived the bond between conscience and *koinonia* (which Lehmann accents as the communal context of Christian conscience) although Luther was mainly concerned with motivational transformation and Calvin was strongly oriented toward structural transformation. Lehmann cites Luther's *Lectures on the Psalms* as evidence that he transcended the tragic conscience which was his arch enemy and perceived the interchangeability of heart and conscience even though he elsewhere called conscience "evil beast" and "wicked devil."[44] (No wonder the Catholics think Luther was negative on conscience.) He speaks of it in Psalms as the place within where we live with God as man and wife.[45] In his "Treatise on Christian Liberty" as well as in other writings he illumined the free conscience, bound in service to neighbor.[46]

It was Calvin, though, who most incisively captured Paul's position in *The Institutes of the Christian Religion,* Book III, where he integrally relates conscience and Christian liberty. For him Christian liberty involves (1) rising above the law and shedding concern for righteousness through it, (2) voluntary obedience to God's will in place of bondage to the yoke of legal obligation, and (3) freedom from obligation in matters of indifference in themselves. He equates good conscience with integrity of heart.[47]

In the covenant tradition and the prophets, in Jesus and Paul, in Luther and in Calvin, Lehmann believes that "the stress falls on a total personal response, 'from the heart,' not primarily through a faculty of judgment [as in the Thomistic tradition], but to what God is doing in the world to make and to keep human life human." In appropriating these resources Lehmann is claiming that conscience is bond rather than bind or bent.

> God's doing, by word and act, provides for man's doing, by word and act, a context within which the directional requirements and the complexities of decision-making can be meaningfully conjoined. In this context, the conscience is fundamentally not a faculty of judgment but a living personal bond between God and man and neighbor. This bond is at once the focal point of sensitivity to what is human and the spring of all right action.[48]

Lehmann does far more than point to resources in biblical and Reformation understandings of conscience. His own contribution provides significant assistance to reformulation. In his development of conscience as the fulcrum of man's humanity, the bond between self and God and between self and neighbor, he presents both a positive appraisal of conscience to balance Lutheran negativism and a relational view of conscience to offset the substantial version which characterizes much Roman Catholic thought. Lehmann treats Christian conscience in terms of the total self's response from within the nexus of the Christian fellowship to the humanizing action of God. For him the central consideration must be the self's need for radical reorientation or renovation of its springs of motivation through the grace of God. Whereas man cannot close the gap between the ethical claim and his ethical actions by the strenuous flexing of his moral muscles, God's forgiving grace bridges this gap. Where bootstrap efforts lead only to despair or pride, to the polar slaveries of heteronomy or autonomy, God's gracious action in Jesus Christ brings an integrity of conscience which issues in theonomous freedom. His covenantal conscience in free obedience is inseparable from responsibility if not synonymous with it.

Lehmann is so concerned to accentuate the indicative of God's gracious action and to undermine the legalisms of man's attempts at self-justification that he neglects the importance of the divine imperative and leaves his *koinonia* ethic vaguely defined at best. Ethical sensitivity is exalted appropriately, but at the expense of ethical content for conscience. Still we are richer for this contemporary American theologian's union of responsibility and freedom in a covenantal conscience which is seeking to act in correspondence with the reality which has been made manifest in Christ and is present in his church.

The writing of the late Dietrich Bonhoeffer on conscience and responsibility reveals many of the same concerns one finds in Lehmann. Though writing more in the Lutheran law-gospel tradition, Bonhoeffer voices the same dissatisfaction with Thomistic faculty notions of conscience and the same need for the self-justifying conscience of sinful man under law to be redeemed in Christ. Through Christ the self knows that good conscience which is faith and that union of freedom and obedience which is responsibility. In the German thinker's work, however, we encounter an ambivalence about conscience which is objectionable because it is rooted in an assumption that man is conscientious because he is fallen.

Bonhoeffer speaks effectively of the union of conscience and responsibility in Christ, but he so identifies conscience with man under sin and law that an irreducible tension remains between conscience and responsibility even when they have been united in Christ. Certainly, the conscientious Christian is always both justified and a sinner, and ambivalence is quite in order with regard to his conscience. In Bonhoeffer, though, there is more than a hint that the ambivalence remains to the extent that he is conscientious rather than to the extent that he is still a sinner. The young martyr's treatment of the meaning of responsibility offers many possibilities for a positive doctrine of conscience had he allowed *conscience* on the hallowed ground which seems mostly to be reserved for *responsibility*.

Whereas responsibility as he conceives it encompasses all of life as the Christian seeks to do God's will, conscience has more to do with what is off-limits, with what will destroy the integrity of the self, with what is prohibited or permitted. Conscience integrates the self but does not seem to obligate to God and neighbor. Responsibility proves the will of God in the situation; conscience recalls the rules. In responsibility one is freed from bondage to conscience rather than called to conscientious action. Conscience can even be a barrier to responsibility. Conscience appears doomed to confront the self with law rather than with neighbor; it seems to constrain more than to command.

Much of the time, Bonhoeffer apparently finds it virtually impossible to dissociate conscience from its form in two ethical stances he opposes. The first is legalism, which uses the more or less constant and codifiable contents of conscience in absolutistic and self-justifying ways. The second is existentialism, which in its non-Christian forms makes conscience the call to authentic selfhood, with man's potentialities affording the sole resources for answering. This, too, constitutes attempted self-justification. The first has obedience without freedom; the second has freedom without obedience.

Ambivalence emerges when the unity of the self, to which conscience calls, is constituted in Christ and the origin and goal of conscience is no longer law, but the living God and living man. Although the irreducible tension remains and conscience will cut short responsibility at the limits of guilt-carrying ability, there is an ultimate unity between conscience and responsibility because Christ is both Lord of conscience and model of responsibility. In Christ one is freed (from conscience?) to heed the call to responsibility without insecurity, and the conflict of a divided conscience is overcome. The tension finds a dialectical unity in him. A preserver of personal integrity and a reminder of the ground rules for human life are needed, and conscience is both.

There are many promising avenues in Bonhoeffer which lead to a more positive doctrine of conscience than his ambivalence allows, and his very ambivalence toward conscience is a

needed caution sign along the way due to man's persistent
sinfulness. The corporate stress in his strong doctrine of the
church, his extension of responsibility beyond one's station in
life to universal community, his recognition of the wounded
conscience occasioned by divided loyalties, his connection of
conscience and integrity with unity constituted in Christ, his
cognizance of the significant uniformity in the content of conscience as presentation of fundamental features of the law of
life—all of these and other strains of his thought are the stuff of
which an understanding of Christian conscience comparable to
the incisiveness of his treatment of conscience under the fall
and compatible with his treatment of responsibility in Christ
might be reconstructed.

A living German ethicist who stands in the same tradition
with Bonhoeffer and exhibits some of the same assets and lia-
bilities is Helmut Thielicke. His *Theological Ethics* drives
home a relational or dialogical view of man, rejecting Catholic
version of the *imago dei* as being resident in man's "indestructible rationality." This basic approach is clearly evident in his
rejection of "ontic thinking" which makes conscience an "objective component to which appeal can be made."[49] As in the
case of Bonhoeffer, Thielicke sees conscience entering the picture with the knowledge of good and evil which accompanies
man's fall. A cleavage is introduced in the ego as two conten-
tious parties confront each other.[50] Torn between good and
evil, man is pitted against himself. Conscience under this law of
sin is a lawyer whose services may be retained on either side of
this cleavage. As St. Paul suggests (Romans 2:15, 16), it may be
the prosecuting attorney, accusing the self of its guilt before
the law, or it may be the defense attorney defending the conscience against God through rationalization.

For Thielicke the conscience under law and the conscience
in the gospel cannot be put under the same rubric. Christ totally destroys the old conscience in order that the self-pacifica-
tion or denunciation of the sinful self may be replaced by the
conscience comforted by God which is faith. Now God defends
the self against conscience instead of conscience's defending the

self against God.[51] Thielicke is attacking that kind of thinking about conscience as a point of contact for the gospel which would present it as a neutral container. For him the conscience of sinful man is not transformed or enlightened or corrected; it is destroyed.

This utter discontinuity between the old conscience and the new is the overly radical working out of a valid objection to ontic or neutral container thinking; it overlooks the continuity between common grace and saving grace which is present with the discontinuity and leaves conscience in an extremely negative position even in salvation. Thielicke's contribution is still substantial, however, despite these reservations. His analysis of the dialogical character of selfhood and of the inner cleavage occasioned by sin are major assets in the capital campaign we have undertaken.

Gerhard Ebeling is still another German Lutheran who stands in the law-gospel tradition, but he stands in contrast to the utter negativism about conscience we have been noticing and makes an incisive case for understanding conscience as in some sense a point of contact, or, as he puts it, a hermeneutical principle. He appropriates Martin Heidegger's later emphasis on the linguistic nature of existence and is able to free himself of the individualistic bent of much existentialist thought, including that of his mentor, Rudolf Bultmann. For him conscience refers to the forum structure of existence, to its linguisticality. Conscience is the place of occurrence of the word-event. In sin (under law) the self as conscience is questioned, asked where he is, confronted with his finitude. The gospel or word-event speaks to this condition and frees man from answering for himself for responsibility to God and to others. Ebeling calls conscience the hermeneutical principle because it designates that linguistic structure of the addressable self which is the point of contact for the gospel's communication. Thus he is able to avoid what Thielicke calls "ontic thinking," affirm a dialogical view of man, and still say more about conscience as point of contact than Thielicke can bring himself to say. His position will receive greater elaboration in the next chapter.

A final recent or contemporary Protestant resource which must be mentioned here and which will also be treated in more detail in the next chapter is the thought of H. Richard Niebuhr. Drawing from a variety of extra-Christian resources, especially the social psychology of George Herbert Mead and the existentialist theology of Martin Buber, Niebuhr presents his own creative version of social selfhood. Like Thielicke he speaks of a dialogue within the self, but his dialogue cannot be subsumed under the headings of conflict and antagonism. He describes the way in which "the other" in the self's inner dialogue represents the self in the community and the community in the self. For him what distinguishes a self is the community to which it is ultimately responsible and the center of value of that community. In the case of the Christian community, its representative in the self is Christ or the Holy Spirit, pointing to God as center of value and to universal community as the scope of the self's responsibility.

The radical juxtaposition by Lehmann, Bonhoeffer, and Thielicke of the Hebraic-Pauline-Reformation concept of conscience as integrity of heart over against the Roman Catholic concept of conscience as the faculty of moral judgment sets the traditional differences of approach between Catholicism and Protestantism in bold relief, but it could easily occasion our writing off the contribution of thinking in the Thomistic tradition to our reassessment of conscience. Without denying the differences or the deficiencies on either side it is sheer folly to bounce from the Psalmist to Jesus to Paul to Calvin to Barth and think we have tapped the resources of the Christian tradition. Protestants could at least do the Catholic tradition the favor of learning what it actually is. Although there is much present agreement in popular usage of the term *conscience* by Catholics and Protestants, the traditional differences have persisted among the theologians. Reporting on the 1963 *Ecumenical Dialogue at Harvard*, David Little, Yale professor, writes, "It was, generally speaking, in the discussion on conscience that the terms 'Protestant' and 'Catholic' seemed to make sense in identifying different positions."[52]

The position of Scholastic theology since the thirteenth century is succinctly summarized by the Catholic scholar, Charles E. Curran: "The Thomistic school distinguished conscience, the judgment of the practical reason about a particular act, from *synteresis*, the quasi-innate habit of the first principles of the moral order. St. Bonaventure placed more emphasis on the will especially with regard to *synteresis*."[53] Protestants have frequently ignored this latter voluntarism in the Roman tradition, and Bernhard Häring is in these days trying to avoid the reductionism of either a cognitive or a voluntaristic sort. He is stressing that *synteresis* involves both a disposition toward the good and a knowledge of it which lies behind the individual acts of conscience and that both this knowledge and this disposition have to be understood in terms of love. Man tends toward his chief end or highest good. He is disposed toward an image or order or union for which he was made. To read Häring is to gain appreciation for the riches of the teleological thrust of Thomas and Augustine.

The Catholic tradition also offers aid on the matter of the guidance of conscientious judgment. In its concern to get at the springs of motivation and to tie all Christian ethics to God's justifying grace, which occasions man's believing response, Protestantism has often failed to help the moral agent as he reflects on murky matters of moral choice. The heirs of the Reformation have thought primarily in terms of the total self's relation to God in alienation or in forgiveness. Speaking of good or bad conscience thus points primarily to a bonded or broken relationship rather than to a judgment about the rightness or wrongness of a past or future action in light of natural and divine law. The Protestant focus has been transmoral; the Roman Catholic-Anglican emphasis has been on morality in specific instances. Each has something to learn from the other.

Casuistry became a bad word; and aside from a few legalisms, the faithful were left to flounder. It has often been a matter of not doing enough and doing it badly in the spirit of the football player who said, "I may be little, but I'm slow." In Protestantism we have generally eschewed guidance for fear of being prescriptive in a casuistic way and then felt forced to guide sporadically when we found ourselves unable to be anything but prescriptive in a pietistic way. Even if Catholicism has attempted at times to cover too many eventualities in its moral guidance, Protestant reaction has often left the self ill-equipped to cope prudently with any but the most obvious eventualities.

A more recent phenomenon than the pious prescriptions of Protestantism, which left the politician or college administrator or executive in corporation or union to operate with little more help than a thought for the day or the suggestion that they reread the Boy Scout law, is the social issues switch. As Paul Ramsey has pointed out, some of the denominational and ecumenical statements on social issues have gotten quite specific, but at the same time any kind of assistance in other areas of moral choice has been avoided ardently.[54] Ramsey's contention, expressed most recently in his book *Who Speaks for the Church?*, is that the church must resist the temptations to make specific pronouncements except in the most extreme circumstances and stick to the cultivation of a societal ethos and the informing of the statesman's conscience. One can readily agree that glib pronouncements by church bodies have been woefully naive on occasion and at times so specific as to fault all other courses of action as "unchristian." Despite Ramsey's keen interest in political problems and issues, his extreme reticence could lead the church to exercise such caution against making mistakes that its assessments of issues would not risk venturing beyond the platitudinous. The church's errors have more frequently been those of omission despite the marred record of commissions by commissions and conferences.

To point out the need for guidance is not to call for an answer-book morality, either for personal morals or public policy. Rather the fear of being prescriptive, which is a well-founded fear, can prevent the church from being instructive. In some areas of moral choice the church is speaking, but in others its silence is deafening. It is no wonder that several highly intelligent industrial managers could conclude with regard to a certain group's study of a pressing decision that since there were no matters of legality, honesty, or kindness involved it was not a moral issue.

There is Catholic wisdom under the heading of *prudence* or the "tact of conscience" in the situation of which Protestants could well become aware. Richard Baxter's bidding has apparently been laid to rest even in his own Reformed traditions.

> Prudence is exceeding necessary in doing good, that you may discern good from evil, discerning the season, and measure, and matter, and among divers duties, which must be preferred.—Therefore labor much for wisdom, and if you want it yourself, be sure to make use of them that have it, and ask their counsel in every great and difficult case. Zeal without judgment hath not only entangled souls in many heinous sins, but hath ruined churches and kingdoms, and under pretense of exceeding others in doing good, it makes men the greatest instruments of evil. There is scarce a sin so great and odious, but ignorant zeal will make men do it as a good work.[55]

Bernhard Häring's moral theology is an impressive Catholic resource on all these counts. He appropriates his own Thomistic tradition both critically and creatively. He draws on both psychological and existentialist thought as he sets moral selfhood in the context of God's word and man's response, of grace and freedom. His view of selfhood is wholistic (avoiding the rationalistic pitfall of Scholasticism), personalistic, and dialogical. He espouses an ethic of responsibility, which he distinguishes from an ethic of law and an ethic of self-realization or self-perfection. He is at pains to insist that the Christless conscience is a flameless candle in need of God's gracious word although he also insists on designating conscience as an indestructible disposition toward the self's good. Like Lehmann, he makes good conscience inseparable from integrity of heart and accents the role of the church as the context of Christian conscience, but of course his view of ecclesiastical authority is very different from that of any of the Protestant thinkers. He describes in detail "the tact of conscience" or the way prudence should function in decision-making and offers guidance about specific issues. At the same time he is able to avoid many of the casuistic pitfalls of those moral theologies in his tradition which have severed their connections with dogmatic theology. He never completely resolves the conflict in his thought between conscience understood as a moral faculty and conscience in the context of word and response, and he gets too prescriptive at points in an attempt to tie Christian conscience to some content amid the winds of situationalism. Yet he makes great strides toward a wedding of conscience and responsibility and opens rich possibilities for ecumenical dialogue.

To these resources from the Christian tradition, past and present, must be added insights on conscience and responsibility from outside it. We have noted several examples of indebtedness among the chosen contemporary Christian contributors to philosophers and social scientists who do not identify themselves with any religious tradition, and this appropriation is both desirable and inevitable if Christian thought is not to exist in a vacuum by limiting itself to dialogue "within the family." The approach espoused here, that of Christ as transformer of culture, values "secular" insights. Seeking to avoid both the theological incest which promotes feeblemindedness and the obsession with being "in" which succumbs to mere like-mindedness, this stance listens with the critical ears which have heard a Word that provides criteria for assessment of words from secular thought.

The provision of a survey of all the resources from contemporary thought which hold promise for a reassessment of conscience would require that the writer be a recent Renaissance man, which he undoubtedly is not, and that the reader be prepared to read an additional volume of this study, which he undoubtedly would not. A few fleeting references will have to suffice.

Existentialism, as has already been implied, has rendered a valuable service in certain respects. Writers in this stream of thought have helpfully repudiated certain psychological reductions of human behavior to a matter of tension reduction and the satisfaction of urges.[56] In any discipline which concerns it-

self with man, some view of human existence is consciously or
unconsciously presupposed, and whereas behaviorism has made
the self analogous to organic and mechanical processes, existentialism has provided a corrective to such reductionisms with its
analyses of care and conscience.

Although existentialists of the Sartrean variety err as grievously on the side of the individualistic autonomy as the B. F.
Skinnerites do on the side of behavioristic heteronomy, the
thought of the Jewish theologian Martin Buber stands out for
its social existentialism. His influence is probably greater than
that of any other one thinker in making our age aware of the
dialogical nature of selfhood. His juxtaposition of the "I-
Thou" and "I-It" relations has passed into the linguistic currency a generation. In *Between Man and Man,* his statements on
"responsibility" and "the single one in responsibility" furnish
searching analyses of the self's answerability when addressed.[57]
He distinguishes the routine conscience from the "unknown
conscience in the ground of being" or "the conscience of the
'spark' " which is heard only in the moment of decision when
the self recognizes his responsibility as distinct from his group's
and answers what he deems to be divine speech.[58]

Psychoanalytic theory is often individualistic also, but there
are rich mines of meaning in *gestalt* psychology and sociology
for understanding the interpenetration of the self with other
selves and with its several social groups. Erik Erikson, a psy-
chologist whose writing on the development of the self from the
womb to the tomb deals sizably in matters of identity and responsibility, provides wealth which needs tapping on the self's
psychological needs and social interrelationships.[59]

The patron saint of linguistic analysis, Ludwig Wittgenstein, is a relevant philosophical source of insight from outside
the existentialism-phenomenology camp. Wittgenstein opposed
the notion of a self inside the body, a Cartesian "hangover,"
and dispelled the idea of mental activity as private. Herbert
McCabe writes of him, "It was, I think, the greatest achievement of Wittgenstein to show that the mental world is not private. To have a mind is not essentially to have a means of with-

drawing from the public world into a secret world of your own, it is to have a special way of belonging to the public world, it is to belong to a community."[60]

Another corrective to any tendencies to make the I too private comes from the thought of Hannah Arendt. Although she is dealing more with epistemology than with ethics in this case, she posits, in *The Human Condition*, that sociality is the fundamental human condition. She indicates with respect to verification of our cognitions that "the presence of others who see what we see and hear what we hear assures of the reality of the world and ourselves."[61] She says further, "Each time we talk about things that can be experienced only in privacy or intimacy, we bring them out into a sphere where they will assume a kind of reality which, their intensity notwithstanding, they never could have had before."[62] For her, thought is an inner dialogue in which another is represented in the self. The parallels between this view and H. Richard Niebuhr's depiction of the dialogical character of moral selfhood will shortly be apparent.

Miss Arendt's writing on totalitarianism likewise bears testimony to her concerns with the loss of identity through the breakdown of meaningful social relations. As she explains in her tome, *The Origins of Totalitarianism*, the soil was prepared for totalitarianism by the rendering of certain segments of society superfluous (first the nobility, then Jewish state bankers, and so forth). During the era of imperialism, the nation-state, which had been the sheltering organization of Western political society, disintegrated. The social hierarchy of class which had stratified Europe broke down. Civil wars occasioned migration and uprootedness and the loss of nationality, and with it the loss of rights. Man became isolated in political life because he no longer belonged to representative groups and classes, and uprooted because he had no place in the world guaranteed by others. Without these identifications the conditions necessary for the realization of democratic freedoms were gone. Atomized mass man was produced, ripe for leadership by the mob and for the fictions of totalitarian propaganda and ideology. Without going into the intricacies of totalitarianism it should be recalled that under both Hitler and Stalin the attempt was made to substitute a party parallel for every social grouping, to break down family, church, occupational loyalties, and to create an atmosphere of distrust and suspicion in which every person felt alone. Each person had his own spy in effect because as Helmut Thielicke has expressed it, "Even a conscience that has been won remains uncontrollable and is therefore an uncertain quantity, as long, that is, as it continues to be an alert, living conscience."[63] Brainwashing is of course the ultimate tactic short of extermination for handling this stubborn phenomenon.

From a number of directions, then, a privatized notion of the self has been called into question, and it is this dialogical line of approach which we wish to pursue without falling into the heteronomous pitfalls of the socially "adjusted" or collectivized conscience on the other. Two theologians who have contributed greatly at this point are two who have related conscience and social responsibility to the point of equation. These men are Gerhard Ebeling and H. Richard Niebuhr. While Dietrich Bonhoeffer, Paul Lehmann, Häring, Joseph Fletcher, and others have related conscience and responsibility closely and suggestively,[64] Ebeling and Niebuhr stand out when it comes to analysis of the structure of social selfhood and connection of this analysis with an understanding of conscience. We turn now to a more detailed look at their renditions of conscience and responsibility in terms of the ego-alter dialectic (Niebuhr) and the forum-structure of existence (Ebeling).

3 Conscience and Responsibility: Toward a Dual Definition

The isolated individual may be wise or foolish; he cannot be moral or immoral. The Atheistic Debauchee upon a Desert Island is not liable to moral censure. It is then our membership in society that makes us capable of morality, and it is consciousness of that membership that endows us with a moral sense. This is the condition of the possibility of obligation—of any sense of "ought"—and of the particular form of Good which is distinguished as Moral Good or Right. And if this is so, it becomes a matter of quite primary importance for the purpose of ethics that we should find out what we mean by Society and by the individual's membership in it.[1]

H. Richard Niebuhr: The Ego-Alter Dialectic

James Gustafson points out that for H. Richard Niebuhr social ethics had at least three starting points: Christian revelation and faith, analysis of the self, and understanding of social processes and institutions.[2] The second focus is seen most clearly in his posthumously published lectures, *The Responsible Self*, but examination of his 1945 journal article, "The Ego-Alter Dialectic and the Conscience," reveals that his concentration in the 60's was only the fruition of his concern in the 40's. In both instances we find him relying heavily on the work of philosophers and social scientists. Though he evolves a distinctive position of his own, his sources for his position range from G. H. Mead, Harry S. Sullivan, O. H. Cooley, and Josiah Royce on the social psychological and philosophical side to Martin Buber on the existentialist theological side. Here his difference in approach from Barth and Bonhoeffer is apparent. For example, whereas Bonhoeffer feels called upon to show that *responsibility* and *vocation* correspond to New Testament concepts,[3] Niebuhr is admittedly taking the concept *responsibility* from such disciplines as psychology, social psychology, and history. He does state that the idea of moral life as responsible offers one key to understanding the biblical ethos.[4]

Because he believes that man is more basically a social being—living in dialogue, responding to action upon him—than he is a citizen living under law or a maker seeking to achieve an end, Niebuhr uses *responsible* as his central description of the self. As he sees it, man's sociality is primordial, not derivative.[5] While man is both citizen and maker, experience bears out, for Niebuhr, that his responsibility in community with other selves is fundamental. The moral life is participation in a conversation we enter as it is in progress. The image of man as responder does not deny but includes the contributions of the other two images which correspond to an ethic of the right (deontological) and an ethic of the good (teleological) respectively. The "ought" ethic and the "end" ethic have been the dominant models in Western ethical theory. Without denying the validity of either, Niebuhr feels that the model of answerer in a dialogue is more basic and can include, not preclude, the other two. Man the maker in teleological ethics understands himself as related primarily to ideas and ideals. He is a rational being knowing objects of reason first and knowers secondarily. This stance is highly individualistic because it relates itself to the ideas of the others rather than to the others. Likewise the image of man as self-legislator in deontological ethics makes other selves secondary. Relation to them is always under a primary relation to law. From this perspective, conscience appears to be the center of the self, and the knowledge of this conscience is "knowledge of law and of myself in relation to law, not knowledge of other selves, or of myself in relation to those selves."[6] Citing Mead, Sullivan, and Cooley, Niebuhr makes this latter relation primary whereas the legal preoccupation compromises it, if not confounds it. Response to rules or principles and ends or goals is secondary. Basically the self lives in response to other selves and in remembrance and expectation of their actions. The self's reflection on itself is mediated through its dialogue with others. "I experience my guilt not as a relation to the law or to an ideal, but to my companions. And I experience it not as my relation to timeless being but as relation to a continuous interaction that has gone on and will go on through a long time,"[7] Niebuhr states.

Niebuhr's point is illustrated well in the case of the worrisome conscience of Frank Alpine in Malamud's *The Assistant*. He felt guilty about having taken part in the holdup of Morris Bober's store and about taking money out of the cash register when he began working there, but not because stealing was so abhorrent. It was because he had hurt one who was now a friend and the father of the woman he now loved.

> And Helen made him feel, from the way she carried herself, even when she seemed most lonely, that she had plans for something big in her life—nobody like F. Alpine. He had nothing, a backbreaking past, had committed a crime against her old man, and in spite of his touchy conscience, was stealing from him too.
>
> . . . .
>
> It was a funny thing about that; he wasn't really sorry they had stuck up a Jew but he hadn't expected to be sorry that they had picked on this particular one, Bober; yet now he was. He had not minded, if by mind you meant in expectation, but what he hadn't minded no longer seemed to matter. The matter was how he now felt, and he now felt bad he had done it. And when Helen was around he felt worse.[8]

Niebuhr summarizes his view of responsibility in this sentence:

> The idea or pattern of responsibility, then, may summarily and abstractly be defined as the idea of an agent's action as response to an action upon him in accordance with his interpretation of the latter action and with his expectation of response to his response; and all of this in a continuing community of agents.[9]

At least four elements are comprised in the moral life: (1) response to prior action, (2) interpretation, (3) accountability, and (4) social solidarity. Of the fourth element Niebuhr writes, "Personal responsibility implies the continuity of a self with a relatively consistent scheme of interpretations of what it is reacting to. By the same token it implies continuity in the community of agents to which response is being made."[10] It is significant that after his brief discussion of Niebuhr's view of responsibility, Joseph Fletcher, in his book entitled *Moral Responsibility*, latches on to the first element, responsiveness, as the most important. He mentions that Niebuhr did not treat freedom as sufficiently as he would have had he lived and then proceeds to neglect grossly the other three elements of responsibility himself. Nowhere is he more deficient than at the point of understanding the self in its social solidarity, and accountability is grievously slighted as well.

Thus Niebuhr proposes a relational (not relative) ethic of the "fitting" or "appropriate" as more adequate than teleological or deontological ways of conceiving ethics. "All action . . .," he writes, "is response to action upon us."[11] "In our responsibility we attempt to answer the question: 'What shall I do?' by raising as the prior question: 'What is going on?' or 'What is being done to me?' rather than 'What is my end?' or 'What is my ultimate law?' "[12] Goals or laws are not goods in themselves. Their value is in relation to persons and to the Eternal Thou.[13] The core concern is not that we ought to be responsible or that the goal is responsibility, but that we live in response to action on us. The question should be, " 'To whom or what am I responsible and in what community of interaction am I myself?' "[14]

Niebuhr locates the distinctiveness of a Christian reading of what is being done or what is going on in the faith that God as Creator, Judge, and Redeemer is acting on us in all action upon us. Monotheistic responsibility means responding to all actions upon the self in such a way as to respond to the One who is somehow active in all events.[15] "Thus," as Gustafson puts it, "Niebuhr moves with ease between a view of the nature of man's moral existence to a view of the nature of God's being and presence as an active one."[16]

In his 1945 article, Niebuhr begins by singling out one element in the highly complex experience often referred to as conscience in its broad connotations. He does this because he feels that concentration on one element or motif, including its interrelations with others in the complex, could be the first step toward a better understanding of the nature and function of conscience. The distinguishable element he chooses is an inner moral dialogue, "the phenomenon of a duality in the self in which one is judged, counseled, commanded, approved, or condemned by an *alter* in the *ego*."[17] Precedent for such a focus is found in Socrates' *daimon*, Kant's inner court with self as judge and accused, and Adam Smith's division of the self as agent and impartial spectator.[18] This kind of analysis, however, needs completion and correction because of confused and inadequate versions which have appeared. Two of these confusions are (1) the duality which splits the self into higher (reason) and lower (passion or emotion) parts and (2) the attribution to the spectator–agent duality of only an "as if" status.

Having defined these confusions Niebuhr delineates two distinctive movements, both of which take place in the moral life and into both of which reason *and* emotion enter. These are: "(1) the [internalized individual-society] conflict between the more and less socialized, integrated, and rational organizations of ideas, drives, and sentiments within a self; and (2) the dialectic in the self between an other and the self in which the future or past acts of the self are subjected to scrutiny."[19] The second movement, the ego-alter dialogue, is more fundamental, Niebuhr asserts, than the first, in which idealism has been interested, but the empiricists' analysis of it needs purging and developing to avoid higher-lower self-confusions.

The initial step is to ask who the self is, who the other is, and what the relation is between them. Niebuhr proceeds to invoke George Herbert Mead's insights on "the generalized other" to shed light on the problem. He agrees with Mead that man experiences himself only indirectly and by way of the standpoints of individuals in his group or from the "generalized standpoint of the social group as a whole."[20] To become a subject to oneself, one first becomes an object to himself just as others are to him, and he does this by assuming the attitude of attitudes of others toward him.

In addition to Mead, he also cites Martin Buber's primordial "I-Thou" and "I-it" relations which precede any atomistic "I" or atomistic object.[21] The Jewish existentialist-theologian comes up with results strikingly similar to those of Mead and his followers who are evolutionary, biocentric, and behavioristic. Niebuhr indicates, "Using Mead's language we might say that Buber points out how the I in I-it relations is not a reflexive being. It does not know itself as known, it only knows; were it not for the accompanying I-Thou situation it would not know what it knows. It values but does not value itself or its evaluations."[22] Niebuhr's indebtedness to Buber is discernible in his advocacy of "social existentialism" as opposed to the abstract individualistic existentialism of Søren Kierkegaard. He writes in *Christ and Culture:*

> Though the voice of conscience is not the voice of society, it is not intelligible without the mediating aid of others who have heard it. It is not in lonely internal debate but in the living dialogue of the self with other selves that we can come to the point where we can make a decision and say, "Whatever may be the duty of other men, this is my duty," or, "Whatever others do, this is what I must do." Were it not for the first clause—"Whatever others think or do"—the second could not follow. So it is with the confrontations by Christ. . . . The Christ who speaks to me without authorities and witnesses is not an actual Christ; he is no Jesus Christ of history. He may be nothing more than the projection of my wish or my compulsion; as, on the other hand, the Christ about whom I hear only through witnesses and never meet in my personal history is never Christ for me. We must make our individual decisions in our existential situation; but we do not make them individualistically in confrontation by a solitary Christ as solitary selves.[23]

Buber presents fewer problems for Niebuhr than does Mead, with whom he has some strong disagreement despite their unity on the social mediation of self-knowledge. He first argues with Mead and like-minded social theorists because "too often they conceive of the self as living in a single society."[24] Not only does the self they present lack any relationship to an

Other who transcends any and all of man's communities, but all man's human communities are lumped into a single "generalized other." In *The Philosophy of the Present,* Mead opens himself to this criticism in his wording of his position:

> We assume the generalized attitude of the group, in the censor that stands at the door of our imagery and inner conversations, and in the affirmation of the laws and axioms of the universe of discourse. . . . Our thinking is an inner conversation in which we may be taking the roles of specific acquaintances over against ourselves, but usually it is with what I have termed the "generalized other" that we converse . . .[25]

Against what Niebuhr calls a "composite photograph which the self makes of the associates in his society,"[26] he urges that the self lives, not in one, but in many communities which are not the concentric circles which they are sometimes assumed to be. "The self does not deal with one 'generalized other' only but with many, and not all its 'others' are 'generalized.' "[27] In self-knowledge and self-judgment, one may meet representatives of family, professional society, and religious community, and for the Christian there is still more to be said than that:

> As a Christian he judges and examines himself "in the eyes" of Jesus Christ, who is not a representative of a society so much as the spiritual organizer of a community. The "I" may meet and confront itself through a representative or epitome or center and source of the universal community, that is, through God as the most general other or as the God of revelation.[28]

Niebuhr contends, in criticism both of Adam Smith's "*impartial* spectator" and Mead's "*generalized* other," that the Thou one encounters as a social self is "not a composite other but yet something general in the particular."[29] The self does not have innate knowledge of its own continuity and self-identity as it moves from one I-Thou relation to another. The larger context or pattern which informs one's response to another is the constancy experienced in the several encounters one has had with the other. In the context of past action upon me and responses to me as well as of expectations of future responses, my present action is delivered from being mere reaction. The particular actions are parts of a continuous discourse which sets the context. "I live," concludes Niebuhr, "in the presence of, and in response to, a Thou who is not an isolated event but symbolic in his particularity of something general and constant."[30]

The Thou not only has an attitude of constancy toward me, he does so with other members of the community to which we both belong. "The social self is never a mere I-Thou self but an I-*You* self, responding to a Thou that is a member of an interacting community."[31] In my experience of conscience, the other from whose viewpoint I judge myself is not some vague figure abstracted from the individuals in society (as Mead seems at times to imply), rather I am dealing with constancies in the responses to me of various individuals in that community, and it is these constancies which enable my interpretation of action upon me. If law be used to describe these constancies, it must be understood as analogous to natural law "in the modern or perhaps nineteenth-century sense" rather than to "obligatory, political law."[32] Law is thus understood here as accepted structures of relationships which have evolved from a society's common life. The political concept obscures my dealing basically with men, not laws, but to fail to recognize constancies is to forget that we deal with others in a predictable order or context or pattern. The upshot of Niebuhr's analysis is that the self exists neither in response simply to isolated other individuals nor simply to a vague, abstract "generalized other." In between these poles is the life of the self in community with other selves. In his own words, "my conscience represents not so much my awareness of the approvals and disapprovals of other individuals in isolation as of the ethos of my society, that is, of its mode of interpersonal interactions."[33]

The others in whose presences the self knows itself are, to a large extent, not freely chosen despite the attempts we make at evading the judgments of some others and our preoccupations with the judges we think we want to please most. The others come unwanted to judge and direct often, and the self is not able to make them approve by rationalization or dilution of their judgments. These others are not impartial either. They are interested in various beings, values, and ways of living, depending on what "other" it is. The other's judgment of the self is disinterested because of the interest in the cause which is common to self and the society the other represents.[34]

A question has been put to Niebuhr by Julian Hartt, among others, as to whether the self is so exhaustively defined by his relationships as not to enjoy "any being, value, and power outside of these relations."[35] However, Hartt himself believes that in the end Niebuhr agrees "that persons cannot be resolved or reduced into nexus of relations, for then the relations are left without ground and without meaning."[36] For Niebuhr the dominant reality is the One beyond the many in whom all being is grounded and given meaning, and it is precisely due to an inescapable relation to that One that a person is not reducible to the nexus of his human relations.

Gerhard Ebeling: Man's Co-humanity to Man

Gerhard Ebeling was known first as a follower of Rudolf Bultmann, but he is now blazing trails of his own, previously in "the new quest for the historical Jesus" and more recently in the discussion which has been labeled "the new hermeneutic."[37] His writing in the area of Christian ethics in general and concerning conscience and responsibility in particular is brief and scarce, but very significant. Relying more on the later Heidegger than the earlier writings which heavily influenced Bultmann, he presents human nature as being fundamentally linguistic.

Ebeling's emphasis on the "linguisticality" of existence is founded on Heidegger's understanding of language as being coming to expression. Man is being's spokesman. As James Robinson explains,

> The subject matter of which language speaks is primarily being. It is man's very nature to hearken to the call of being. . . . In this way language is located at the center of

man's nature, rather than being regarded primarily as an objectification of an otherwise authentic self understanding [as is the case in Bultmann]. For man's nature is defined as linguistic, in that his role is to re-speak, to respond, to answer, the call of being.

. . . .

. . . Man is where being's voice is heard and given room. Man is the loud-speaker for the silent tolling of being.[38]

For Ebeling, what man is as man and the world is as world in the full and final sense can only encounter us by word. Man is questioned by his existence, and this awareness of being questioned is the point of contact to which the gospel speaks. Conscience is the questioning of the self. As he states it, "For conscience is the question 'Where?' knocking at man's door, and by conscience that question is decided to the effect: in prison or in freedom."[39] Thus it is for Ebeling the hermeneutical principle, the ground where the seed must take root. Conscience refers to an addressable self.

Without getting involved at this point with Ebeling's contrast of conscience under law and in the gospel, we can delineate what he understands by conscience and how it relates to man's linguisticality or forum-structure. Ebeling rejects individualistic notions of conscience as the function of a withdrawn inner life. "Conscience does mean man as bearer of a proper name";[40] it does point to the uniqueness of each person. However, the unique person cannot be abstracted legitimately from existence. Human nature, the world, and God are rightly seen only as dimensions of one of them—not as separate themes. The world, which means not the physical universe but the sum of the self's experiences of reality, should be spoken of only in relation to conscience and thus to man and God. The three come together in conscience:

> What we are concerned with in conscience is not a legal code, not individual instructions on this or that, *but man as a whole*—and hence not an authority where morals are concerned, but the defining of man's place where the decision is made on his personal being that lies beyond morality. But above all, where conscience is concerned, the

relation of man to God would be spoken of in the right way only if the world were not left out in doing so.[41]

Why the description of conscience as a place of meeting precludes its being a moral authority we fail to see, but the main point Ebeling is making still stands.

Man may be known apart from conscience; "yet it is only in relation to conscience that the human nature of man makes itself known in truth."[42] In like manner, we partially know experience apart from conscience, but the experiences of reality in their wholeness as "world" are only known in conscience. Neither "world" nor human nature are encountered as a question of conscience unless God is encountered as *the* question in a radical sense. Through word-event in conscience then, man, world, and God are brought together as they should be and transformed to concerns of faith with God as *"the* absolute concern of faith."[43] What man is as man and world is as world in the full and final sense can only encounter us by word.

As Ebeling conceives it, "Man is a matter of conscience in two senses: he is ultimately conscience, and he ultimately concerns the conscience."[44] He is ultimately concerned with the question of himself, and he is the self who is questioned and called to respond. Conscience points up a duality in the self. Conscience is both event (of being questioned) and act (of being responsible), both call and answer. These insights lead Ebeling to view conscience as crucial for the understanding of the relation between dogmatics and ethics.[45] Although faith and morality are distinct, they are united. Whereas religion tends to separate the holy and the profane, the believing conscience sees God, man, and the world properly, as a unity.[46]

The importance of conscience for Ebeling is now apparent. Man does not have a conscience; he is a conscience. "Conscience," as we have quoted Ebeling before as saying, "is a matter of coming to expression of man himself."[47] Conscience is an inclusive term for man the questioned, the called, the responder, the answerer, the linguistic being. "To identify with ourselves is to answer for ourselves. Thus existence is fundamentally word-event [and also conscience] and can be answered for only in word-event."[48] Even though conscience is the precondition for understanding what is meant by the word *God,* the voice of conscience is not as such the voice of God. In the standing before oneself which characterizes man as conscience, one is not already before God. However, his awareness of finitude or his openness to question involves openness to the question of God.

In contrast to Bonhoeffer, who sees conscience entering human life as sin's unsilent partner, Ebeling argues for an ontological interpretation of conscience and against a view which makes salvation the abrogation rather than the transformation of human nature. "For how," he asks, "can anything be *understood* as a state of unsoiled or perfect human nature, if it appears to run counter to what we say ontologically of man, or at all events is averse to the possibility of being stated in ontological terms?"[49] Ebeling, in other words, is insisting that the image of God in man is not utterly destroyed by the fall and that the image refers to man as conscience or responder.

Not a code of general truths, not an inner law in the sense of inborn ideas, conscience as inner law is "the question mark branded irradicably on man."[50] It asks man about himself, but gives no speeches. Silence is the mode of its speech. The content varies with the individual depending (1) on his concrete situation, that is the location and relationships which constitute the setting for his hearing the word and responding, and (2) on all the training he receives in understanding this situation in which he stands. "The call receives its content by being heard."[51] Niebuhr's naming of interpretation and social solidarity as elements in responsibility are recalled by Ebeling's position here.

In an article entitled "Theology and the Evidentness of the Ethical," the Zurich professor explicates responsibility, which for him is the fundamental ethical category and which further clarifies his understanding of man as conscience. He examines four compulsions in man as man which are need-creating conditions of human existence.[52] They occupy the place of natural law in Ebeling's thought. First, there is the compulsion to act.

With time on his hands, man is summoned to action which passes time, puts in time, or fulfills the time. As Ebeling words it, "Man is summoned to action for the reason that he is summoned to himself [by conscience according to descriptions of the summons which have been previously noted]. For it is still an open question who he really is. Man has not come to grips with himself. He must therefore go beyond himself as one who outwardly acts and forms."[53] The question is whether he can realize himself by words, and the answer is that he cannot. His creative action or work in response to the fear of annihilation or the awareness of transcience cannot satisfy the radical claim which time places upon him.

Secondly, there is the compulsion to surrender. To gain, one gives oneself up in response to the given. The mother gives herself over to her child, the child to his play, the craftsman to his work. The moral claim which is placed upon the person by the other self, the activity, or the work is not that he give himself up for the purpose of self-realization or other reward, but rather that he assume responsibility for the other person or task. Surrender is the way a man accepts responsibility for what is entrusted to him. "The commandments," Ebeling states, "are the call to assume responsibility for what is given."[54] The gifts of father and mother to be honored and the lives of neighbors to be preserved make claims which are prior to and more basic than commandment. "The gift arouses surrender."[55] On the basis of this gift-surrender relationship, Ebeling shows how "conscientiousness, responsibility, gratitude, joy, trust and love [are] basic phenomena of ethics."[56] Ebeling's position here parallels Niebuhr's response to prior action and is strongly reminiscent of Buber's as expressed in this quote about responding to the situation as it happens to you. "We respond to the moment, but at the same time we respond on its behalf, we answer for it. A newly-created concrete reality has been laid in our arms; we answer for it. A dog has looked at you, you answer for its glance, a child has clutched your hand, you answer for its touch, a host of men moves about you, you answer for their need."[57] The pressing moral problem arises when this relation between gift and surrender is disturbed and the question of the limits of surrender presents itself. When sacrifice is demanded, one has to discover where the limits of his commitments are. The conscience cannot be allowed to become or remain provincial, but one can take on too much responsibility.

Coming to the compulsion to put right, the German theologian understands himself to be moving from the forecourt of ethics to the specific sphere of ethics, the distinction of good and evil. It is now the threat of evil which demands a response. Ebeling calls good that which puts right or makes good an evil situation or condition. He avoids the individualism which plagues much existentialist theology by insisting that isolated man is only a ghost of a man and urges that ethical reflection should always begin in a situation of violated relationship where the call of love comes:

> The true and only serious urge to ethical reflection is the fellowman who is already wronged, the one already humiliated and offended, whose toes we have stood on perhaps precisely by failing to allow him to come near us, encroach upon us, hurt us, drag us into his suffering. Hence it accords with the evident fact of human relations having been already impaired when we set out from the compulsion to put right and interpret that compulsion as the call to love our neighbor.[58]

The claim of love is radical because it extends beyond family, friends, nation, or any partial group to humanity, and because it makes putting right a personal responsibility.[59]

The fact that the radical demand of co-humanity or responsibility for humanity is beyond us occasions the necessity of laws, customs, and civil order so that society may persist despite the absence of personal responsibility. As in the case of the first two compulsions, the self is driven beyond his own resources. Putting right the failures of one's responsibility for all of humanity or overcoming the evils of man's inhumanity to man does not get to the root distress. The man who is a "menace" to his neighbors and himself needs to be put right within. This only comes by another's taking our part, being responsible for us so that we are freed from menacing ourselves.[60]

The final compulsion corresponds to Niebuhr's element of accountability in responsibility; it is the compulsion to render account. For human society to continue, this accountability must extend beyond our answerability to each other, man to man. "The universality of responsibility is shown by the fact that we know ourselves urged to conscientiousness even when we are subject to no one's control and no one could call us to account."[61] Even thinking is a moral obligation, for it "means rendering oneself account."[62] Man's responsibility to God is not, for the Zurich professor, a separate responsibility but "the truth, depth, and radically concrete form of man's single responsibility."[63]

From these compulsions of man, Ebeling concludes that responsibility, with "its implied forum-structure of being compelled to render account—to oneself, to another human authority, or to God,"[64] is the fundamental ethical category. Conscience and responsibility turn out to be inseparable, if not interchangeable. Man exists in word-event and thus in conscience. In his linguisticality he is defined as addressable, responsible, or accountable, because he is spoken to before he speaks. He is acted upon before he acts. He is historic because history has happened to him. Before he is spoken to, he has the potentiality, but not the ability, to speak. When Ebeling posits that "co-humanity is a condition of the possibility or responsibility,"[65] he is saying in another way that man is basically a social being. Furthermore, "Co-humanity is not to be abstracted from co-worldliness."[66] We do not communicate in a vacuum. What is communicated lies outside us. We speak of something; word leads *to* something. The world is always present in world event.

The similarity between Niebuhr's model of man as answerer or responder and Ebeling's concepts of linguisticality and responsibility should by now be apparent. One could wish that Ebeling had tied linguisticality to the kind of social understanding of selfhood which we find in Niebuhr, but Niebuhr's responsible self does find a counterpart in Ebeling's co-human self as word-event. Their contributions are by no means identical or coextensive, but they are complementary and capable of harmony. Ebeling's hermeneutical focus causes him to concentrate often in areas other than Niebuhr's steady insistence on the interpenetration of the self and its communities, but they both present *conscience* as a forum where the self, its neighbors, and its God meet and as a term for referring to a reality about moral selfhood to which *responsibility* speaks most significantly. Ebeling's connection of co-worldliness with co-humanity resembles Niebuhr's depiction of the self relating to singular and plural others in the presence of a third, whether it be nature, nation, cause, party, or God.

On the fourth compulsion to render account, of which Niebuhr speaks as "the anticipation of reaction to our reaction,"[67] their marked likenesses are well illustrated. Ebeling emphasizes, "No deed, not even a deed in the form of spoken word, can be left to itself. It becomes complete only through what follows it."[68] A person can have many attitudes toward his own word/deed—identification with it, rationalization of it, silence which speaks regret, or lack of comprehension of one's actions. The necessity of follow-up is the self-realization of being in and being known by one's fruits. "For what has really and ultimately to be accounted for is man himself."[69] Both the exercise of responsibility and accountability for one's responses are included in responsibility, and the giving account lasts as long as life. Ebeling affirms, "For the court of conscience there is no statute of limitations, and no discharged cases. Because man himself is the object of responsibility, the responsibility suit, including that of responsibility for the past, goes on as long as he lives."[70]

With the compulsion to give account, once more the ethical points beyond itself to problems it cannot handle. Man needs to be put right by love that springs from freedom and enables freedom. The answer must come in the occurrence of liberating love which relieves him of the hopeless compulsion to answer for himself and the world.[71] For the fourth time, Ebeling has thus indicated that ethical problems point beyond ethics for solution.

Formulation of a Definition

The resources have been reviewed, and the two major contributors have been heard from. We move now to capitalize on these contributions by formulating our own definition.

The Greek word for conscience, *syneidesis,* and its Latin equivalent, *conscientia,* suggest the root meaning "knowing with" oneself, intimate self-knowledge. This etymological exercise gets a different twist by various theologians. Lehmann suggests "knowing in relation." Tillich uses "being witness of oneself"[72] as root understanding which ties consciousness and conscience closely together. Carl Michalson's position is that the God-given conscience is not a moral judge but a gauge of spiritual health, and he gives this rendition: "To 'know yourself together,' or whole, is the responsibility of the conscience."[73] While the original Greek notion emphasized condemnation for nonconformity with an external order, Lehmann is stressing the relational connotation of heart as a personal bond between two. Michalson and Tillich reflect the existentialist stress on self-actualization or self-realization.[74] These definitions are somewhat disparate; but with the transformation of the Greek impersonal order to a covenant God, a reconciliation of the several emphases may not be impossible if conscience is conceived basically as self-knowledge in relation to other selves following Niebuhr's lead.[75]

The writer understands conscience to include both the "must" of the internalized social authority and the "ought" of the mature self who evaluates in light of its own self-image, to use Allport's distinction.[76] We take into account both authoritarian and humanistic conscience, both submission for the sake of social adjustment and creative expression of integral selfhood, to borrow Fromm's categories.[77] However, it is on the self-image which has been genuinely appropriated by the person, not merely imposed upon him, that attention is focused here as we consider conscience in terms of inner integrity of heart, following in the train of John Calvin. The voice of conscience is the summons to wholeness, to realization of one's self-image, to true selfhood. Without subscribing to Fromm's version of humanistic conscience, we can, nonetheless, employ his general definition of conscience as "the reaction of our total personality to its proper functioning or dysfunctioning; not a reaction to the functioning of this or that capacity but to the totality of capacities that constitute our individual and human existence."[78]

Whether this phenomenon is presented deontologically as obligation or teleologically as the tendency or striving toward an ideal, or whether this reality is experienced more in terms of intellect or emotion or will or varying combinations of these, there is an inner pull in the self toward integrity, wholeness, and self-realization. Even when social sanctions are withdrawn and at times in opposition to these sanctions, there is a call to responsibility, to accountability, which characterizes man as a moral being who keeps and breaks commitments, and makes decisions in terms of what is right or wrong for him. What distinguishes one man's conscience from that of another is not only or even primarily whether or not he has allowed his biological drives or his immediate pain and pleasure to relegate integrity to the background. The watershed is rather at the point of that in which one finds his integrity or wholeness.

Where does the self's ideal self-image originate? What characterizes it? If conscience be stated in terms of responsibility to oneself as Heidegger does, to what self is he responsible? To what does he feel ultimately obligated? What is his main aim or intention in life? To use Lehmann's refrain, "What makes human life human?" When Emil Brunner contends that conscience primarily has nothing to do with the voice of God,[79] he is right in that conscience is not innately or universally the voice of the God and Father of our Lord Jesus Christ. But conscience can in another sense be called the voice of god. The Niebuhrian question concerns what god the self serves, or what one takes to be of supreme worth. What is the center of value of the self which gives it its ultimate worth and purpose and norm? What is the self's final court of appeal? Amid the clamor of the voices from which the self hears what roles its varying societies would have it play, which is ultimately obeyed? Men may have many objects of loyalty, but to the extent that they have integrity, there is one ultimate loyalty, whether to interest group or family or nation or company or church or God, which constitutes the self's center of value.[80] In Robert Penn Warren's *The Cave,* the situation of the rebellious preacher's son Isaac Sumpter is thus presented: "He was himself, and there was no God. No, he was not himself. There was no God and there was no self."[81] Change the capital *G* to lowercase *g* and our point is made.

The person's ideal self-image is integrated around a center of value; it is also shaped and defined within a social context of identity. Daniel Callahan, in his astute article, "Self-Identity in an Urban Society," writes: "To have a self-identity is to have a sense of psychological and social context. A psychological context insofar as one can connect in some coherent way one's remembered past, experienced present, and envisioned future, and a social context insofar as one can relate oneself to other persons and the context of their lives."[82] The center of value of the self does keep it from "going to pieces" psychologically, and one of the dimensions of the integrity it gives is a coherence to the self's past, present, and future. Callahan's other context, the social one, brings into bold relief the dependence of self-identity on social relations. As Erik Erikson expresses it, "ego-identity 'connotes both a persistent sameness with oneself (self-sameness) and a persistent sharing of some kind of essential character with others.' "[83] The problem of the juvenile delinquent is one of "ego-diffusion." He suffers from uncertainty about how he regards himself and how others regard him, the former as a result of the latter.[84] To put the matter in terms of integrity, rather than identity, fidelity to the self requires knowing who the self is.

Personal integrity must be set in the context of social integration. Man is basically or primordially a social being and only derivatively a striver after an ideal or an observer of laws. Self-knowledge is socially mediated and so is knowledge of God.

Ideal self-image and experiences of "ought" are derived from life in the family and the person's other communities in which he develops. There is an interpenetration of the self and its various societies with each influencing the other. The external laws or expectations of a group and the conscience of the member of the group interact upon and support each other. Groups develop styles of life and come to embody allegiances to certain norms and certain images of men. What the self is constitutes a response to what it sees reflected in the social other which it encounters not only outside itself, but within the self; for the boundaries of the self reach into the community and the boundaries of the community reach into the self, a fact which Richard Niebuhr clarifies brilliantly. What one seeks to become reflects the facets of the self-image demanded by one or another society which are internalized and, in the mature, either rejected or consciously appropriated. Societies disintegrate apart from some corporately recognized version of what it means to be human.

John L. Thomas, in his article "Conscience and a Pluralistic Society: Theological and Sociological Issues," provides an insightful analysis of the way in which an image of man underlies the ethical system which a society develops and of the dependence of the system's continuation on a persistent commitment to the image of man it originally embodied.

> In the final analysis, every ethical system implies a conception, or image of man, the human agent. Considered in its broadest sense, this image involves a set of beliefs concerning man's origin, his relation to space and time, the essential qualities of his nature and consequently his orientation toward his fellowmen, society, and the world of nature and finally, his life purpose or destiny, that is the desirable terminus of his development or fulfillment in the cosmic order as he defines it. In other words, although all men recognize the quality of oughtness in human conduct, the specific contents of this oughtness are necessarily related in the final analysis, to the distinctive image of man people cherish. This does not imply that significant social symbols, endowed with ethical qualities, may not persist as cultural residues in any ongoing social

system. However, to the extent that these residues are not related to the prevailing image of man, they gradually cease to be operative or may summarily be rejected in situations of crisis.[85]

According to Robert Bolt in his Preface to *A Man for All Seasons,* the ethical poverty of our time is found precisely in this lack of an image of man without which the self loses its identity. He writes:

> We think of ourselves in the Third Person.
> To put it another way, more briefly; we no longer have, as past societies have had, any picture of individual Man (Stoic Philosopher, Christian Religious, Rational Gentleman) by which to recognize ourselves and against which to measure ourselves; we are anything. But if anything, then nothing, and it is not everyone who can live with that, though it is our true present position. Hence our willingness to locate ourselves from something that is certainly larger than ourselves, the society that contains us.[86]

No wonder Wylie Sypher finds a "loss of the self in modern literature and art."[87]

Jesus, of course, has been exalted as the representative man *par excellence* in the Christian community, but he seems to most like an outdated model today. Daniel Callahan remarks,

> . . . It is almost impossible for a contemporary man to model his life on Christ's. Most of us will marry, few of us will be carpenters, hardly any of us will try to collect disciples and then speak to them from boats or on mountain tops. As an urban people there is hardly anything in the setting of our lives which finds a ready parallel in the setting of Christ's life; physically, culturally, psychologically, it is totally different.[88]

What pattern if not Christ? On what new model is he to be traded in? Man the redeemer, says Gabriel Vahanian in his *The Death of God,* but what image of man, it is hard to say. "Man now is what Christ, according to the New Testament, was to the world. He is the new redeemer, the meaning-giving center of this post-Christian era. . . . Just as it was difficult ever to be sure of precisely what the will of God entailed, so it is equally difficult to determine which image of man is going to govern man's responsibility for this world."[89]

Not only do people need an acceptable image of what it means to be human; they also need visible and accessible identity models. The search for identity in our time is at least in part a search for representative men and women to identify with. When there is an absence of at least somewhat "representative" leadership, social cohesion is threatened. It is significant that candidates they could identify with got many disenchanted young people back into American political life prior to the last election.

The existence of visible and accessible identity models is of course not just crucial for college students. Adolescents ape the speech, dress, work goals of an adult model, and adults in less specific ways model their lives after some hero-figure, whether religious or secular. In the day of the anti-hero, who is one to follow today?

John Fry's considerations of the role of the self's images in pre-ethics emphasize the hidden reservoirs which provide resources which make responsible action possible. A person's pre-existent images of himself, his marriage, his church, his world, his God, inform and mobilize action. Conflicting images or perverse images immobilize the Christian who is called to act in certain ways. If he cannot see himself in such a role, he is paralyzed by conflict of that image with the one he has internalized from his communities. Writes Fry, "What is needed before . . . the strictly conceptual relation of love to justice, or justice to law, or law to love is set down, is assurance that the Christian public has an overflowing abundance of images that are specifically recallable onto their internal screens. Then the image-making that is inevitably the prelude to responsive action will be appropriately pre-inprincipled, or, turned inside out, pre-contextualized."[90]

Rollo May, the psychoanalyst, makes a similar point. He posits that symbol and myth, though different (myth being more inclusive), function the same psychologically. "They are man's way of expressing the quintessence of his experience—his way

of seeing his life, his self-image and his relations to the world
of his fellow men and of nature—in a total figure which at the
same moment carries the *vital meaning* of this experience."[91]
His lament is that no symbols or myths today seem to have the
compelling power of meaning—not even love and success symbols, much less the symbol God or "the stars and stripes" or the
myth of Adam. The breakdown of the central symbols in modern
Western culture has occasioned a confusion of the individual's
self-image and a crippling of his capacity to transcend the
immediate concrete situation from the perspective of some
larger context.[92] The prominence of psychotherapy as a special-
ized activity rather than as a normal and spontaneous function
of family, education, and religion testifies to the disintegration
of symbol and myth. The integrating concepts which inform
thought and inspire action have been diffused if not destroyed.

The importance of social context for the understanding of
a person's self-image and his "knowing with" himself, which is
basic to conscience, cannot be overemphasized. The self's
inner dialogue springs first of all from the self's relation to other
selves and to the corporate "others" of its communities. There
is a duality in the self because it is social, and this person always
speaks in reply to, if not always in agreement with, his societies.
Integrity then is not individualistic but relational. If a person
hears Thoreau's "different drummer" contradicting a society
of which he is a part, he may be responding to a community
rather than a crowd, but his conscience is still in some sense
social. The laws and goals which his conscience defends grow out
of personal relations. The self reaches beyond itself and beyond
the conscience of the community, but what it reaches toward
has invariably been pointed to if not achieved or exhausted in
one of its communities. Reinhold Niebuhr has claimed that
communities do not have a conscience in the full sense in which
the individual does because of the individual's greater self-
transcendence,[93] but he also argues against any notion of "purely
individual" conscience:

> . . . The most effective opposition to tyrants in recent de-
> cades has come not so much from isolated individuals,
> but from individuals whose conscience was formed by po-

litical, scientific, cultural, and religious communities. There is in short no dimension of existence in which the individual is purely an individual and is not in need of either material or spiritual or moral support from some community.[94]

It is certainly true that the desired interaction between a society and a self can turn out to be only an authoritarian dictation. Much of the earliest shaping of the self-image of the child is by way of "musts" which are not chosen as obligations but enforced as requirements. It is against the background of such heteronomous oppression that Freud, Fromm, and others with a psychoanalytical orientation have belittled the subconscious, oppressive, authoritarian superego which internalizes the sanctions of society and have elevated the creative, expressive autonomy of the self. Although Fromm urges autonomy on behalf not of individualistic man but of universal man,[95] others in his camp and such existentialists as Heidegger and Sartre have sometimes exhibited a more individualistic bent as they have accented the call to cease being one-like-many in the security of averageness. It is their claim that assumption of responsibility for oneself in untrammeled uniqueness is the way to authentic existence. However, from a Christian perspective the answer to heteronomy is not autonomy. The answer to an ethic of adjustment is not a preoccupation with self-realization. As Roger Shinn writes,

> In a Christian humanism man discovers his own humanity via the grace he knows in Jesus Christ, via a free obedience and an obedience that frees, via a sharing in the death and resurrection of Christ. He is not making the concentrated and resourceful effort to be himself; he is celebrating the gift of life and freedom.[96]

Life in response to gift and evil, to borrow from Ebeling, or to single and corporate others, to borrow from Niebuhr, takes on a different style from life in quest of personal fulfillment as the primary objective. There is no freedom without responsibility to something which transcends the self as it is; and because man is a social animal, his responsibility is to others and for others as well as to himself.

It is the individualism and egocentrism of pure autonomy

which occasioned Bonhoeffer's ambivalent assessment of conscience as barrier to responsibility[97] and prompted Brunner's
assertion that conscience and legalism are inseparable.[98] Man's
integrity or self-realization is properly neither heteronomous
nor autonomous. For the Christian it is constituted precisely in
his responsibility to God for neighbor rather than in making his
responsibility for himself his chief end or in submerging himself
completely in his societies. There can be a difference between
self-interest and egocentricity. We are contending that one's
integrity is not centered rightly when its center of value is the
self, but that self-interest can be good or bad depending on
what self one is interested in becoming.

A person belongs to many groups. The more complex the
culture in which he participates the more selves he is expected
to be. The process of group integration is the process of conscience formation, but the self cannot be all the selves his groups
demand. His integrity comes when he makes membership in one
community and commitment to its center of value the court
of appeal for the clamor of the voices he hears within. (This
involves the question of authority which is the focus of the
next chapter.) This court must be a matter of conscious choice
unless the self remains in the childhood of submission to an
alien authority forever, and that too is a choice. Growing up
involves a transformation of conscience from the burden of
social constraint to the bidding of personal conviction, but it
is shared personal conviction. Peter Bertocci, Richard Millard,
and A. C. Garnett all make this the distinction between "automatic conscience," meaning the conditioning of the traditions
in which one is reared, and "critical conscience," referring to
the autonomous maturity which can take or leave the dictates
of the automatic conscience, depending on which is discerned
to be the better course of action. We are not satisfied with their
choice of the adjective *autonomous* but the distinction is helpful.[99]

The upshot of our reassessment is that conscience should
be an inclusive word encompassing the total self, not just a
piece of the self, as it functions in light of a self-image it has

accepted, and that it should be a relational word with responsibility as a companion concept. Conscience refers to a duality in the self—a self to which some center of value gives integrity—an integrity which includes the self's inner dialogue —a dialogue in which the self's communities interpenetrate the self just as the self is part of the communities—communities which share loyalties to the objects of loyalty which give integrity and identity both to the community and to the selves in community. We are concerning ourselves with a triangle of responsibility or fidelity or integrity: (1) integrity within the self or responsibility to oneself, (2) responsibility to other selves who have been "taken to heart," and (3) loyalty to a cause (Royce) or center of loyalty (Niebuhr) or ultimate concern (Tillich) or a transcendent source of meaning and purpose which gives integrity to the self and which may unite a given community or give integrity to all man's community ties. Although men are, more often than not, polytheists who are pulled in many directions by their loyalties, wholeness of life depends on having a center of value which gives integrity to the whole of the relational self's relations. By *conscience* we are referring to the person's self-awareness, thought and action in response to his situations in life (which include Ebeling's time, gift, evil, and one's own word-deeds)[100] and in response to the trio of responsibilities we have described.[101]

4 Conscience and Community Authority

Unless I am convicted by Scripture and plain reason—I do not accept the authority of popes and councils, for they have contradicted each other—my conscience is captive to the Word of God. I cannot and I will not recant anything, for to go against conscience is neither right nor safe. God help me. Amen.[1] (Luther at Worms)

But why did a man [Sir Thomas More] so utterly absorbed in his society, at one particular point disastrously part company from it? How indeed was it possible—unless there was some sudden aberration? But that explanation won't do, because he continued to the end to make familiar and confident use of society's weapons, tact, favor, and, above all, the letter of the law.

For More again the answer to this question would be perfectly simple (though again not easy); the English Kingdom, his immediate society, was subservient to the larger society of the Church of Christ, founded by Christ, extending over Past and Future, ruled from Heaven. There are still some for whom that is perfectly simple, but for most it can only be a metaphor. I took it as a metaphor for that larger context which we all inhabit, the terrifying cosmos. Terrifying because no laws, no sanctions, no *mores* obtain there; it is either empty or occupied by God and Devil nakedly at war.[2]

Howard Levy knew what was demanded by medical ethics and international law. He came to know that Special Forces aidmen systematically violated these demands. And he knew, too, that according to the Geneva Conventions, he, as an individual doctor was *responsible:*

. . . .

And because Howard Levy's conscience would not permit him to be an accomplice to what he knew or sincerely felt to be crimes, he was persecuted, prosecuted, and convicted.[3]

Seventeenth-century England was a capsule of Christendom in its time when it comes to the continuing debate on the question of conscience and authority. It was generally assumed that God was the supreme authority for conscience, and it was a virtually universal conviction that what Milton called in *Paradise Lost* "my umpire conscience" was the moral monitor of every man. The conflict raged over the mediator of divine rule. Rationalists such as John Locke trusted that the intellect was sufficient guide to God's truth. Roman Catholics and Anglicans such as Richard Hooker looked to church tradition (which for the Romans was represented by the papacy), scripture, and right reason. The Puritans, such as Richard Baxter, with their Calvinistic background exalted scripture as confirmed to the believer by the Holy Spirit. Sectarians stressed Spirit more than scripture and in some cases Spirit apart from scripture. The Quakers emphasized the "inner light" above the outer word, and they were not alone in their dominant accent on personal religious experience.[4] The discussion continues today as ecumenical dialogue occasions reexamination of the relation of the objective (scripture and church) to the subjective (experience and individual conscience), of the Bible to tradition.

The Crisis of Authority

If there is a lessening of the old rigidities, there is also evidence that for many the openness is too little and too late. The withdrawal of Charles Davis from the priesthood of the Roman Catholic Church, the writings of Michael Novak and Daniel Berrigan, the participation of hundreds of priests and nuns in the Selma-to-Montgomery March despite the orders of their Alabama Archbishop that they stay home and "tend to God's business," the marriage movement among the clergy, and the birth-control rebellion are signs of a growing impatience with the Roman Catholic Church's institutional authority. In Protestantism attacks on and despair of the institutional churches are even more widely spread and widely said.

Meanwhile, whatever authenticity the term *Christendom* ever had has been eroded, and the crisis of authority in the church is mild compared with the suspicion of authority which is growing up in many other quarters. Historians may well suggest in years to come that the slogan of our age was "Let Freedom Fling." On the home front it is often touchy to talk of parental authority. The ghetto dwellers have given up on the urban authorities. There is widespread student rebellion against administrative authority. Exponents of the politics of both "the new left" and "the radical right" decry the "establishment's" authority.

Frustrated by the difficulty if not impossibility of changing America, the new left has grown "allergic to authority," to use a phrase of Christopher Jencks'.[5] Impressed with the removal of the decision-making process from the people whose lives are affected by the decisions, this movement has gone sour on America more because of the way decisions are made than because of what the decisions have been. Paternalism in the high places of university administration, governmental bureaucracy, and industrial hierarchy is the object of revolutionary criticism on behalf of "participatory democracy" in all areas of American life. Anyone who opposes "the Establishment" cannot be all bad and therefore one hears expressions of sympathy forthcoming from "the new left" for groups as diverse in ideology as "the radical right" and the National Liberation Front.

In general our open society is freer than ever before of ecclesiastical and even civil authority as dominant and formative forces. Helmut Thielicke captures a prevalent mood when he says of the temper of the times, " . . . any power which lays claim to moral authority, e.g., the Decalogue, must vindicate itself before the bar of my autonomy. Thus the final authority which is binding beyond everything else resides in me, or, more precisely, in my intelligible ego."[6]

Liberation is essential to true humanity, but at least since the French Revolution we should recognize that men just do not continue to live without authority. As André Gide has Michel say in *The Immoralist,* "To know how to free oneself is nothing; the arduous thing is to know what to do with one's freedom."[7] Despite the suggestions of Erich Fromm and other members of Emancipators Autonomous, the human personality abhors a vacuum and being one's own boss can be the worst of tyrannies. Conscience will be taken captive by something. The issues are what master will be served or what norms will be adopted and also whether authority will reign through a sense of responsibility willingly accepted or an enforced restriction resentfully acknowledged. In *The Fall,* Camus' judge-penitent, Jean-Baptiste Clamence, speaks movingly of the untenability of masterlessness.

> At the end of all freedom is a court sentence; that's why freedom is too heavy to bear, especially when you're down with a fever, or are distressed, or love nobody.
> Ah, *mon cher,* for anyone who is alone, without God and without a master, the weight of days is dreadful. Hence one must choose a master, God being out of style. Besides, that word has lost its meaning; it's not worth the risk of shocking anyone.[8]

The abhorrent vacuum which Camus depicts is highlighted in somewhat different fashion by Paul Hessert's reminder that "while one can say that the breakdown of family authority gives the child more freedom to choose his value systems, it may also make him more amenable to the value system of his peers, the education system, or the mass culture that surrounds him on every side."[9] The conformity demands by our school systems and the conditioning we absorb from the mass media are often threats to creativity and molders of conscience to an extent we seldom realize. Thielicke speaks not only of the autonomous ego, mentioned earlier, but also of the autonomous spheres of public life— economic, military, political, and aesthetic—which dislike restraint and often demand subtly that we board their bus and leave the driving to them. Although his prescriptions are sometimes less therapeutic than his diagnoses, Marcus Raskin stimulated an awareness of the heteronomy produced by these autonomous spheres in his 1967 Campbell Lectures entitled *Being and Doing: Decolonization and Reconstruction in American Life.* His hearers and now his readers are pushed to greater admission of the way in which they have been taken in, bought up, and otherwise "colonized" by the imperialisms of the dream colony (mass media), the plantation colony (economic), the violence colony and the education colony.[10] Edgar Friedenburg in *The Vanishing Adolescent* and other writings has described the difficulty the youth has in finding himself in the school systems of America where conformity is at a premium and independent thought and creativity are often discouraged. John W. Gardner in his books *Excellence* and *Self-Renewal* is another perceptive analyst who makes us aware of these quiet conquerors.

One of those who is concerned about the filling of the void left by the decline of ecclesiastical and civil authority is political philosopher Walter Lippmann. He describes a vacuum in the open society at which he says the preponderant majority of Americans have arrived:

> They have found, I submit, that as they are emancipated from established authority they are not successfully equipped to deal with the problems of American society and of their private lives. They are left with the feeling that there is a vacuum within them, a vacuum where there were the signs and guide posts of an ancestral order, where there used to be ecclesiastical and civil authority, where there was certainty, custom, usage and social status, and a fixed way of life. One of the great phenomena of the human condition in the modern age is the dissolution of the ancestral order, the erosion of established authority; and, having lost the light and the leading, the guidance and the support, the discipline that the ancestral order provided, modern men are haunted by a feeling of being lost and adrift, without purpose and meaning in the conduct of their lives.[11]

Lippmann is sure that the void will be filled by something, and he urges that the university must step into the void if disaster is to be averted. With the demise of priestly and kingly authority, "there is left as the court of last resort when the truth is at issue, 'the ancient and universal company of scholars.' "[12] Rather than turn to government or church, we must turn to the university as Lippmann sees it because "the behavior of man depends ultimately on what he believes to be true, to be true about the nature of man and the universe in which he lives, to be true about man's destiny in historical time, to be true about the nature of good and evil and how to know the difference, to be true about the way to ascertain and to recognize the truth and to distinguish it from error."[13]

Lippmann is only one of many who are looking to the university to become a secular equivalent of the church which can communicate some kind of consensus concerning cultural values. Almost no one would crown the university as it exists characteristically today for such a messianic role, but hope abounds in some quarters that higher education can be reoriented to do as effective a job of stimulating the acquisition of wisdom (which "refers to such things as justice, freedom, ethics, and all those profound areas of human endeavor in which we attempt to apply human reason to the problem of living the good life")[14] as it has of spearheading the accumulation of the kind of knowledge which might be designated as science, to use Harvey Wheeler's distinction. An international "Coca Cola" culture is being communicated, thanks to our technological advances, and John McHale of the World Resources Inventory of the University of Southern Illinois is among those who believe that common ideals of justice and respect for human values are no less communicable than soft drinks and TV serials.[15] A global culture is possible. There is talk of a shift from education for problem solving to education to love.

Because the stakes are so high in the effort to find a focus for societal integrity and international consensus, only the cynical will desist from the effort to realize all the potentiality which education offers for man's welfare. At the same time, the assertion by a Princeton dean in a televised interview that the educational transformation and the consensus for which many long would be an act of divine grace can hardly be regarded as completely facetious.[16]

Without asking for the faculty of a university to speak with one voice or denying the importance of institutions of higher learning in the shaping of the man of tomorrow, we would have to cite the often-muddled multiplicity of the multiversity which occasioned Robert Hutchins' now famous designation of the modern university as a group of buildings connected by a common heating plant. Lippmann readily admits that higher education has often been information-oriented rather than knowledge-oriented, but he grounds his hope on the commitment he sees in academe to diligent and free inquiry. Is that commitment enough?

The fact is that college and university professors are and should be committed to values in addition to that of free inquiry. The teacher who is worth his salary has an open mind, but he also has closed his mind, at least tentatively, on a world view, an image of reality, and an ethical stance. If he fails to recognize this himself, he is deluded; if he fails to admit it to his students, he is dishonest. Professor Tiryakian of Duke University wrote in an article entitled "A Perspective on the Relationship of Student and University":

> Students look for positive ideals and values from their teachers . . . If they do not find ideals and values from their teachers, they develop apathy, boredom, or accept ersatz values, from LSD to other forms of extremism. The spirit of nihilism and absurdity is the specter that is haunting the academic setting. It must be exorcized right in the classroom, by a faculty which is passionate in the search for truth, and which will be ready to import its enthusiasm to its students. To present the fruits of our research, and the relation of our research to ideals, values, and the meaning of life, therein lies the source of authentic academic enthusiasm.[17]

The values of one's professors should be a stimulus to self-discovery in the realm of such commitments and not a relief from personal weighing and choosing. The point is that if the university is to become increasingly influential as the shaper of a culture, it does no one a service if the students it produces are sterile in their sophistication. If anything, this eventuality is more to be abhorred than the promulgation of a single-value system by the caricature of the church-related college which is the bête noire of academe. In our zeal for deliverance from pietistic propagandizing, one demon may be exorcized only to have seven others rush into the resultant vacuum. If the vacuum is intentionally filled by articulate and able exponents of seven points of view, health may well result, but the insidious domination of a mentality which feigns neutrality is a fate to be feared.

The Concept of Joint Authority

One of the contributions that Lippmann's article makes is the indication that the recession of tradition-direction does not leave the self with only the options of the other-direction of a domineering society or the inner-direction of the rugged individual, to use David Reisman's categories from *The Lonely Crowd*. When one looks to a community for guidance because he shares the values of that community, the result is neither tyranny nor anarchy. We can be other-connected without being other-subjected. Where authority is acknowledged as well as exerted, there is the possibility of what H. Richard Niebuhr calls "joint authorship." For instance, the authority of the peer group is not formal or official, but it is nonetheless powerful. This is so because the self identifies with peers in a way that it often does not with superiors. Peer-acceptance is valued more than superior approval.

The example of student-faculty-administration relations is also pertinent. When a student feels he or his representatives has had some voice in the setting of policy and the establishing of rules, these policies and rules are viewed very differently than when they are completely unilateral decisions. There is identification with authority, if not participation in it.

Kenneth Boulding explains in *The Image* that "in a successful political process all decisions are interim."[18] The discussion is not closed but modified. In this democratic situation there is authority, but it is not authoritarian domination. "The majority does not rule; a majority decision is simply a setting of the terms under which the minority continues the discussion—a discussion which presumably goes on forever or at least for the lifetime of the organization."[19] The more monolithic and less dialogical a group becomes, the more authoritarian it must be because of the lack of identification of the self with the authority.

In all fields of human interaction there is growing emphasis on "partnership," a concept which presupposes differences of position within a cooperative enterprise but also affirms equality in opposition to class formation. Differentiation of function —yes! Division and hierarchical stratification—no! Thus employees are to be deemed co-responsible partners which is not the case in paternalisms of various kinds. The attempt is being made in many quarters to prevent downgrading of workers to second-class status, by legal safeguards and the insistence that certain benefits are theirs as matters of right, not of managerial concession.[20]

Christopher Jencks makes an interesting assessment of the roots of the antipathy toward authority which is found in "the new left." He points out that the young radicals are largely "children of the 1940's, raised in relatively permissive middle-class homes where authority was supposed to be rational rather than arbitrary."[21] Unlike earlier generations, these youngsters were allowed to challenge parental authority and abuse of power. Parents preferred to rule by consensus rather than coercion. There were limits but these were set by what was reasonable and enforced by the retaliation of rejection or hurt feelings rather than the exertion of physical or economic force. Both parents and children were controlled by the fear of rejection.

Jencks argues cogently that these young people who lacked experience with authority structures based on power have been doubly disillusioned when their uses of reason and their expressions of rejection toward the powers-that-be have not eventuated in a radical and rapid reorientation of American society. It is clearly naive to fail to reckon with the facts of the countervailing centers of power and the inevitable anarchy which sovereignty of a totally participatory democracy in every part of society would bring into being. However, the concern of this movement for mutual trust, equality, and respect for individuality and its suspicion of hierarchy and leadership and discipline must be heard. In this instance as in many others one finds himself appreciating the contention that men are usually more to be valued for what they affirm than for what they deny. What is striking about this analysis of Jencks' is that once people experience an authority which is relational, in which they have a share, which has been internalized, they will never again be satisfied with powerless nonparticipation. With the program of the permissive parents we now hear the voices of the disinherited joined. Shown the possibility of participation in the decisions which shape one's destiny, the poor, the black, and the forgotten are wanting in. Some of them in their frustration employ violence to shake the system, a tactic which is, Jencks indicates, almost impossible for most young middle-class white. Both must face up to the necessities of participation in established political institutions, but in light of their protests, the liberal spirit should never be as comfortable with the status quo as it often has been.

In his article "The Ego-Alter Dialectic and the Conscience," Niebuhr suggests that authorship, which is one facet of the authority issue, is experienced in two senses: "On the one hand the author seems to be the other in the mind, imagination, or consciousness. . . . On the other hand, however, it is the self which judges or commands itself in the presence of the other. It gives a law to itself and unless it did this it would not be a responsible self."[22] The first statement refers to the "Thou shalt not" of God, a god, a parent, a neighbor, or community which is deemed alien to the extent that the self is in rebellion against the self-image the author would impose. The Freudian superego comes to mind here. In the second instance the command is felt to be more personally authored in light of one's commitment to an other. The other is friend, not enemy. The obligation has been internalized to a greater degree. Identification has occurred. Both experiences are part of conscience as Niebuhr understands it:

> Both statements may be true, for the authorship in such a dialectic situation can not be ascribed to the one or to the other but only to the common mind. Thus when the other in the mind is the image of Jesus Christ and the dialectical reflection leads to a command or a judgment, it is possible to affirm either that the self, as a Christian, has

judged or that Christ within has judged, but in truth the authorship of the command or judgment belongs to the society of self and Jesus Christ.[23]

When the soldier feels called upon to make a sacrifice for his nation, it is therefore more accurate to say that "the author is the political society in the self or the self in political society."[24] Against those who make conscience autonomous self-legislation (Kant) on the one hand and those who reduce conscience to the imposition of societal mores (Freud) on the other, Niebuhr is contending that there is authorship which is "joint authorship."[25] Because the representatives of the self's various communities often make their presence felt without invitation or welcome, the autonomous position is illusory, and because, despite the attempts of monolithic societies, the structures and commands in conscience never come from only one source, the reduction of morals to mores is equally misleading.[26] The college student's conscience, for instance, may be addressed by faculty, administration, fraternity or social group, team or interest group, nation (through recruiters and draft notices), church, family, and yet more communities than that.

The sanctions employed by this joint authority on the social self is in the form of exclusion as the wages of transgression. As Jencks indicates about the typical middle-class family, the need to belong is what the joint authority has going for it in its demands. Boulding illustrates with respect to the sanctions imposed by a peer group, "We rapidly learn to order our images in the way that the gang orders them because of the extremely low value we place on exclusion and loneliness. We can bear everything except not to be borne by others."[27] As Richard Niebuhr explains, "In guilt, whether it be guilt before a provincial or a universal other [an exclusive or an inclusive community], the self fears exclusion from a society."[28] Niebuhr then maintains that spiritual and natural societies cannot be absolutely distinguished in this regard because the natural community is experienced inwardly and every spiritual community must have external embodiment. A Christian fellowship must have some kind of institutional expression, contrary to some of the contentions about the church made by Emil Brunner, and a town, insofar as it is a genuine community, has an *esprit de corps.*[29]

The Supreme Covenant of Conscience

Another dimension of the question of authority which Niebuhr illumines is "the court of last resort." To whom or what is one ultimately responsible or accountable? Which of one's plural communities holds ultimate sway over the self? When John Bell Williams, Mississippi segregationist, ran for governor of his state in 1967 using as his slogan "Elect an Independent Thinker," he was not showing much independence. He was only revealing that he failed to support the Democratic ticket in 1964 because he was more dependent on and more dominated by the authority of the ethos of the majority of the white electorate in his state than by the promptings of party. The question becomes one of which speaker is heard loudest and clearest in the stereophonic conscience through the selective listening of the self. The quotation from Bolt at the beginning of the chapter about Sir Thomas More points to his hero's loyalty to the larger society of the Church of Christ, and to its founder, a loyalty which qualified allegiance to the more parochial society. In the case of Dr. Howard Levy, his professional society and the international provisions of the Geneva Convention constituted a higher court than commanding officer or military tribunal or even nation. Although polytheistic itineration from one companionship and thus from one conscience to another is prevalent, if the self does have a final court of appeal, a last resort of responsibility after voluntary or involuntary exclusion from all other companionships, it has a god, "a being on which it is absolutely dependent for its value and one whose judgment it can not deny without denying itself."[30] The voice of integrated conscience then is always the voice of a god, though too seldom the voice of God. To have unity in the self, a person must have one center of loyalty upon which he is absolutely dependent. This is so because, as Niebuhr insists, a belief that there is one behind the many others and that it is God, that "the Universal is divine and that God is universal," comes before subjection to one law, one last court of appeal.[31]

Niebuhr's analysis of the triadic form of life in response is closely related to these questions of authority. What follows simply paraphrases his position. The response of the self is not just to individual Thou's and plural You's, but to that to which all Thou's and You's respond in a community. One triadic relation we have involves a cause. Niebuhr finds Josiah Royce's understanding of the moral life as primarily a matter of loyalty very similar to his own use of the heading "responsibility."[32] Of Royce, Niebuhr writes approvingly, "Instead of thinking of man as realizer of ideals or as obedient to laws he saw him as one who comes to selfhood by committing himself to a cause."[33] A person is associated with others who have the same loyalty and is thus bound both to them and to the center of their common allegiance. This is of course a modern form of Augustine's concept of community as held together by a common object of love, which he expounds in *The City of God*. The cause may be nation, science, religion or a common task.[34]

The third reality in the presence of which we respond to companions is something personal, but it points beyond itself to something transcendent. In dealings with legal codes we relate to judges and lawyers but also to a justice beyond their own grasp or handling of it. The nation as cause represents something beyond it, for which it stands. In the case of a democracy, the relation is not simply to fellow citizens. There is a transcendent reference to humanity, and it seems that the vision includes "not only representatives of the human community as such but a universal society and a universal generalized other, Nature and Nature's God."[35]

Human societies or groups tend to become ends in themselves and to make their good the highest good. But Niebuhr is suggesting that in order to elicit the allegiance of persons in a group, it is nearly[36] always necessary to convince them that what promotes the preservation and progress of the group is coincident with commitment to a goal, norm, or community which transcends the life of that particular society. Reinhold Niebuhr's classic analysis, *Moral Man and Immoral Society*, points out that individuals can rationalize doing for and through a group what is to their personal self-interest when its selfishness would be apparent to them as an individual venture. This does not mean that transcendent commitments are wholly hypocritical. Niebuhr's latest book, *Man's Nature and His Communities,* emphasizes the inclination of the realists "to obscure the residual moral and social sense even in the most self-regarding men and nations."[37] But he characteristically continues to ride herd on the idealists' inclination "to obscure the residual individual and collective self-regard either in the 'saved' or in the rational individuals and groups."[38]

It may be that a group is held together only by mutual self-interest, in which case selfish ends are the highest good which is served by the social alliance. The morality of such a group will be determined by these ends, and its norm could be described as mere reciprocity. A society may be held together by a common loyalty to a cause, such as civil rights, which will lift the norm of group to justice rather than pure self-interest. Allegiance to one's country is usually loyalty to it as representative of values the citizen exalts, whether freedom, justice, capitalism, democracy, or socialism. Common allegiance to a transcendent value beyond any mere contract for the achievement of certain personal aims is what makes a community, and what value is uppermost in the minds of the members and of the community as a whole will, in large measure, determine the quality and style of moral life of the community. Persons bind themselves to others in communities which represent a value or values for them. The authority which one grants the community derives from his allegiance to this third, which is represented by the community and which he connects with his chief end or with some lesser good. The ethos of a group embodies the nature of its bond and of the center of loyalty which unites it.

The Christian community likewise points beyond itself as do its book (the Bible), its tradition, and even its representative *par excellence,* Jesus Christ (Matt. 19:17, Mark 10:18, Luke 18:19), and its ethical guidance. Its ethos is supposed to reflect the nature of the center of loyalty which unites it. The outstanding philosopher of religion, Ian Ramsey, described all human authority as derivative in his sermon on the occasion of his enthronement as Prince-Bishop of Durham Cathedral. As he put it,

> Words, persons, institutions possess genuine authority as and when they are vehicles of a vision, as and when they disclose that which they are meant to symbolize; and in responding to such an authority as this, men find their freedom and life. But when the words, persons, institutions lose their capacity to evoke a vision, when they cease to have disclosure possibilities, then we have the authoritarianism which is bogus, oppressive and destructive of personality.[39]

Biblicism, ecclesiasticism, and legalism are usurpers then of authority which is not their possession.

Paul Lehmann emphasizes that ultimate authority is found in God and that all subordinate authorities are authoritative to the extent that they point to God's will.[40] Bonhoeffer speaks of church authority as derived from the authority of the word in Jesus Christ.[41] Niebuhr refers to "educational" authority. As he explains it, the Bible stands always in triadic relation to the Christian. The church must always be seen beside it, but at the same time the church stands under the authority of the Bible. Holy Scripture has a unique content and function because it contains the story of our faith. It is the source of the church's theology without which there would be no Christian ethics. Biblical authority is, however, fallible, and it is not the kind of exclusive source for Christian ethics which both liberalism and neoorthodoxy claimed, in their respective ways. Its authority is educational in the sense that it points beyond itself, and it is corroborative in the sense that it serves to validate or to correct our own judgments and actions. Thus it informs the Christian conscience, but it does not determine it.[42] Even Jesus Christ points beyond himself to the One who alone is good, his Father. This is Niebuhr's radical monotheism.

Bernhard Häring is, as we would expect, less willing to qualify church authority. As his tradition sees it, the church has been established by Christ as "custodian and interpreter" of the revelation of God's will in Christ.[43] Without compromising the integrity of the conscience enlightened by the Holy Spirit, he emphasizes that the believer can look to the church for sure guidance in ultimate matters. On the basic principles it is infallible. However, the conclusions and applications derived from these basic norms depend on the situation and the limitations and degree of moral sensitivity of the agent. On less than ultimate matters, conflict may legitimately arise between personal conviction and non-infallible ecclesiastical rulings. Still, one should assume the rightness of ecclesiastical authority until he is convinced otherwise.[44] If in conscience one goes against the church in matters where no absolute principle is involved, he should not criticize the church in so doing, according to Häring.

If the Christian's ultimate authority is God as revealed in Jesus Christ, then Bible, church, and representatives of the Christian ethos are subordinate. The Protestant will find it hard to grant even the limited infallibility Häring indicates, especially when he looks at some of the absolutes which have bound the Roman communicant's conscience on matters of birth control or truth telling. We do not know Christ apart from the covenant community, but the community can never be equated with Christ. We have to be wary of a static authority which is possessed in favor of a dynamic authority that is relational. The style of life, the principles, the standards and goals of the Christian community point beyond themselves to the center of value in relation to which they have developed. Neither the Bible nor the church and its teachings is the final authority, but rather the God to whom both should point and under whom both stand.

As there will be occasion to elaborate later, the content of conscience is subject always to the context of God's action and nature. Because this action is dynamic, the content of the response to it should not be solidified into absolutes which take the ultimate authority from the living God. James Gustafson has written, "An understanding of moral life as being related to the living God sits loose to the saddle of all closed rational systems of ethics—Christian or philosophical."[45] Authoritative guidelines can be set forth, but their authority is derivative, relational, and conditional. What is absolute is the bond of love between God and man and between man and man in God. To borrow from Bonhoeffer, "The origin and the goal of my conscience is not a law but it is the living God and the living man as he confronts me in Jesus Christ."[46] Its authority is primarily that of a covenant rather than of a law court or goal.

What Tillich and Lehmann refer to as theonomous conscience avoids the polar pitfalls of autonomous freedom without responsibility for others and of heteronomous bondage with no responsibility for decision. Autonomy is out because integration into the Christian community should make personal integrity and universal responsibility two sides of the same coin. Self-realization is the by-product of servant responsibility, not the goal of the Christian life. Heteronomy is out because the authority is a bond not a bind, a bond of *free* obedience and obedient *freedom*. The authority is the demand of love, a demand with shared authorship, a love which the community has experienced in Jesus Christ as inclusive not exclusive, faithful not fickle, self-giving not self-seeking. The love has been poured into the hearts of Christians through the Holy Spirit which has been given to the fellowship of faith (Romans 5:5). The Spirit of Christ is now joint author with the self for those who live "in Christ" or "in the Spirit" as Paul alternately expresses it. The Spirit in the self and the self in the Spirit bear inner witness to a relationship of the self to God and fellowmen rather than an impersonal law or ideal or self-perfection. This joint authorship is no private matter. It is where "two or three are gathered" that Christ makes his presence felt. The joint authorship of self and Spirit is also the joint authorship of the self in the community and the community in the self.

Verdict Verification

We have emphasized that the Christian community is not an infallible court for conscience, but it must also be underlined that it is the highest human court to which the Christian can appeal. The question, "Which Christian community?", is a tough one. The radical splits both between and within denominations and traditions on such questions as pacifism, integration, civil rights strategies, birth control, capitalism versus socialism are real and apparent. It is also true that non-Christians have often been better counselors to conscience than many Christians. The classic remark of Episcopal Bishop Charles Williams to Reinhold Niebuhr in Detroit during their conflict with Henry Ford I on matters of economic justice is a case in point: "In the weightier matters of social justice . . . there are only two Christians in Detroit, and they are both Jews."[47] And similar claims could often be made for avowed atheists in some situations. The fact remains that one should ordinarily turn to those who share the self's center of value for verification in times of perplexity in ethical decision. No one can make our decisions for us, but what Richard Niebuhr calls corroborative authority protects the self against the rationalization of its whims until they can masquerade as the will of God. Corroborative authority is preventive medicine for pernicious private revelations.

How does one verify his conscientious conclusions? If one's decision goes against everything the Christian tradition has stood for and against the best judgment of contemporary Christians whose stands he respects, he had better think more than twice. Luther thought twice because he was bucking the church of his time, but he found support from that same people's past recorded in its book. The verdicts of the self's inner court are far from inerrant. They are, as Niebuhr suggests, subject to a twofold error. The first is the confusion of one "other" with another "other," for instance, the mistaking of the voice of father or of Southern culture or nation for the voice of God. Thus constant scrutiny of the source of the legislation of conscience is necessary. The second source of error is the misrepresentation of the "other" due to the abstraction of inner from public life.

In this latter case the "other" may be rightly identified, but its sanctions or values may be perversely modified in the filter of our appropriation of them. Men need always to check their versions of Christ or democracy or justice against expressions external to them. They must listen to those with whom they share a cause in the "knowing together with" which is conscience—the Christian community past and present, the democratic tradition, or the legal expression of a society's values. Undue concentration on the inner life can lead to distortion beyond recognition of what they claim to espouse. In Niebuhr's words, "It is equally important [with checking public judgment against private convictions] that internal judgments of guilt and internal injunctions to action be verified by reference to visible and audible neighbors."[48] Some "other" is in dialogue with the self in its judgments, whether it admits it or not, contrary to the feigned moral independence of some individualism. It is the prevalence of such individualism which Catholicism has rightly criticized in Protestantism.

Authority and Ethos

We have said that the nature of love as revealed in Christ is universal and inclusive. The court's sovereign determines its scope. Niebuhr's contention about universal responsibility is not only that the unification of self and community in a universal God expands responsibility to universal community, but that "the responsible self is driven as it were by the movement of the social process to respond and be accountable in nothing less than a universal community."[49] Niebuhr posits that for the radical monotheist, the ultimate person, cause or center of community is God, and all causes and communities are called to push beyond their partiality to responsibility to and anticipation of response from the universal Other and the universal community.[50] There only can the expanding circles of self-transcendence end, in the God above all our gods, in the community beyond all our social, political, national, familial, racial cliques. Here conscience finds its final authority, its universal responsibility, its ultimate Other, its Center of loyalty. The monotheistic and universalistic conscience is the final arbiter in the conflict of conscience due to the plural communities of the self. In Niebuhr's own words: "The societies that judge or in which we judge ourselves are self-transcending societies. And the process of self-transcendence or reference to the third beyond each third does not come to rest until the total community of being has been involved."[51]

Just as teleological ethics moves toward the form of the Good that is the form of the whole and deontological ethics seeks the universal form of law, the ethics of the fitting must move to universal responsibility. Then actions we respond to will be seen in a universal context, and the responses we anticipate will come from representatives of universal community with impartial loyalty to the universal cause.[52]

Richard Niebuhr's brother Reinhold would fill in the meaning of Richard's "movement of social process" toward more universal community to embrace the growing concurrence of national interest and the interests of a culture or of the world in a day characterized by increasing interdependence and the "balance of terror." Contrary to some of his more cynical realist followers, he finds an "important residual creative factor in human rationality"[53] which enables extension of a sense of social obligation beyond the purely parochial. Despite this movement (H. R. Niebuhr's) and this concurrence and rational capacity (Reinhold Niebuhr's), both men recognize not only that the coupling of personal integrity with universal responsibility will not evolve inevitably but that even among the "saved," who have supposedly been redeemed from self-concern, the conflict between narrow self-interest or group interest and larger interest persists, with the latter often losing. This conflict will be examined thoroughly in the next chapter.

A Concluding Statement

Our consideration of the problem of authority in light of social selfhood leads to the conclusion that human authority escapes being authoritarian when it is derivative and dialogical or, in other terms, visionary and joint. Vertically the abuse comes when authority absolutizes itself rather than pointing beyond itself to values which are acknowledged both by the

authority and those who stand under the authority. Just as a
government is in trouble where it contradicts or loses sight or
ceases to enlarge the people's vision, so any authority which
dominates rather than educates is tyrannical. Horizontally there
is a crisis of authority when the authority is no longer author-
ized by joint authorship, when the authority is monological
rather than dialogical. Theonomous community authority is
proposed as an alternative to the heteronomy of a collective
conscience which dilutes or destroys the self's responsibility.
It is the other-directed or collectivized conscience that much of
the current rebellion against authority seeks to dodge. Along
with the current antipathy for other-direction has sometimes
gone a refusal to reckon with other-connection. In a concern
for self-realization there has been a neglect of the demands of
community and a forgetfulness of the inevitability of man's
having some master. It is interesting to note that the contemporary "cop-out" movement, the hippies, is communal, although
its grasp of the obligations of community is hardly sufficient for
permanence or for any group-transcending purpose.

Martin Buber, writing on the theme of community in 1929
in a work entitled *Dialogue,* had something to say about the
extremes of irresponsible individualism and collectivist authoritarianism which is perennially significant and startlingly ap-
ropos to the current scene:

> As in the former [the age of the "youth movement"] all
> songs in praise of freedom were sung into the void, because
> only freeing from bonds was known, but not freeing to
> responsibility, so in the latter [men of the "collective"]
> even the noblest hymns on authority are a misunderstand-
> ing. For in fact they strengthen only the semblance of au-
> thority which has been won by speeches and cries; behind
> this authority is hidden an absence of consistency draped
> in the mighty folds of the attitude. But genuine authority,
> celebrated in those hymns, the authority of the genuine
> charismatic in his steady response to the lord of Charis,
> has remained unknown to the political sphere of the pres-
> ent. Superficially the two generations are different in kind
> to the extent of contradiction, in truth they are stuck in
> the same chaotic condition. The man of the youth move-

ment, pondering his problems, was concerned (whatever the particular matter at different times) with his very own share in it, he "experienced" his *I* without pledging a self —in order not to have to pledge a self in response and responsibility. The man of the collective undertaking, striding to action, succeeded beforehand in getting rid of himself and thus radically escaping the question of pledging a self. Progress is nevertheless to be recorded. With the former monologue presented itself as dialogue. With the latter it is considerably simpler, for the life of monologue is by their desire driven out from most men, or they are broken of the habit; and the others, who give the orders, have at least no need to feign any dialogue.

Dialogue and monologue are silenced. Bundled together, men march without *Thou* and without *I*, those of the left who want to abolish memory, and those of the right who want to regulate it: hostile and separated hosts, they march into the common abyss.[54]

Buber describes that community which goes along with genuine authority: "growing community . . . is the being no longer side by side but *with* one another of a multitude of persons. And this multitude, though it also moves towards one goal, yet experiences everywhere a turning to, a dynamic facing of, the other, a flowing from *I* to *Thou*."[55] Discouraged from any attempt to improve on this as a description of the covenant community as it is called to be, we turn to a consideration of the self's conversion to that community and its divine authority.

5 Conscience in Sin and Salvation

Jesus Christ has become my conscience. This means that I can now find unity with myself only in the surrender of my ego to God and to men. The origin and the goal of my conscience is not a law but it is the living God and the living man as he confronts me in Jesus Christ. For the sake of God and of men Jesus became a breaker of the law. . . . Thus it is Jesus Christ who sets conscience free for the service of God and of our neighbour; He sets conscience free even and especially when man enters into the fellowship of human guilt. . . . The conscience which has been set free is not timid like the conscience which is bound by law, but it stands wide open for our neighbour and for his concrete distress. And so *conscience joins with the responsibility* which has its foundation in Christ in bearing guilt for the sake of our neighbour.[1]

In the Christian tradition the shift from a preoccupation with being good to that union of conscience and responsibility in Christ which enables the self to bear guilt for the neighbor is called conversion. The change from bondage to the self and its societies to theonomous freedom is not a matter of evolutionary development but of revolutionary transformation. The movement from conscience as bind to conscience as bond involves "growing in grace," not just growing up.

This chapter concerns itself with the state of conscience and responsibility and their relationship in sin and in salvation. It will attempt to clarify the sundering of conscience and responsibility in sin and their union in Christ. Employing the categories which H. Richard Niebuhr often used, we shall treat our twin concepts (conscience and responsibility) under the headings of creation, judgment, and redemption.

Creation: Conscience as Call to Responsibility

The approach which was adopted in Chapter II toward the relating of Christ and culture carries important implications for the treatment of conscience under the rubric of creation. The Christ-as-transformer-of-culture stance involves the claim that salvation is not in utter antithesis to creation but is in some sense a fulfillment of it. Grace does not merely add to nature or give it clarification of vision; it corrects and converts it. Yet it does not entail nature's total destruction. It does answer questions of the natural man, even as it reveals that the questions have been asked in the wrong way. Because this view rejects the dualism which puts creation and redemption in separate realms and speaks only of discontinuity between nature and grace, it would insist that the image of God in which man was made has not been utterly demolished by sin. Because, as St. Augustine stressed, all evil is a parasite on good; if there were no trace or reflection of divine intention to be found with men, they would cease to be human. This assertion should not be interpreted as a claim for some indestructible property man possesses which carries the divine likeness such as rationality or knowledge of the good. The point is that as we look at man in his perversity we must remember that it is too simple to call him basically evil. His evil affects the core of his being, but even there he is a good gone wrong—not just slightly wrong but dreadfully wrong.

What this approach implies with respect to conscience is that conscience, too, is a good gone wrong. Bonhoeffer and Thielicke ask us to believe that conscientiousness and fallenness enter human life together. Conscience, it seems, originates with the desire "to be like God, knowing good and evil" (Genesis 3:4, 5). It is so identified with self-justification and the establishment of one's integrity apart from God that there is nothing basically good about man's conscientiousness.

This dualistic fallacy can be attributed to an utter disjunction of nature and grace which dislikes all talk of a point of contact for the gospel in man. It can also be blamed on an exaggeration of the needed distinction between "common grace" and "saving grace." Reinhold Niebuhr attacks the overemphasis on the distinction on the part of the religious community in his latest book, *Man's Nature and His Communities*. He posits that common grace is mediated through man's communities. People do know something about true community from their experiences in some human grouping whether it be family, circle of friends, social action group, or an occupational, political, or national community. Beginning with family, traces of true community give security to the self, freeing it from undue self-concern for social responsibility.[2] Niebuhr affirms that "in genuine evangelical experience . . . the self apprehends a larger system of loyalty and meaning than the common loyalties and commitments which are the stuff of common grace,"[3] and he admits that these common loyalties are often idolatrous. Yet he asserts that the law of love is the basis of all moral life even though it cannot be obeyed by a simple act of the will. We have to be loved into loving, but there is more love around than some theological antitheses between God's love and man's have conceded.

The Thomists, following Aristotle, emphasize man's disposition toward the good, the *synteresis* which tends toward man's chief end. Due to this point of view, Catholic thought is often and aptly criticized for its failure to reckon with the radicality of evil, its lack of emphasis on man's failure to know "which end is up." However, man is a teleological being. He is purposive and intentional, and his identity and integrity are tied up with his purposes and ends. Does the fact that he gets untracked and upended make this dispositional bent bad? We think not.

The Kantians like to underline man's feeling of oughtness or duty. It is true that people often do dutifully what they really do not want to do and that a very self-centered and unimaginative rigidity can grow out of the ethic of obligation. Some would suggest that good acts are those done spontaneously and under no "sense of duty." Our question is whether a sense of duty is so totally on the side of sin. Are love and obligation antithetical? Is the fact that we "dutifully" change dirty diapers at 2 A.M. solely an evidence of sin or is it a part of our finitude and a necessary and good part of our humanity—a good that repeatedly goes wrong?

With H. Richard Niebuhr, we have said that man's being social is even more basic than his being teleological or deontological. According to Lester A. Kirkendall in his article "An Emerging Morality and the College Counselor,"[4] the assumption that man is a social animal by nature is supported by scientific evidence, which is gaining ever-widening acceptance. He states, "His nature, in fact his very survival, demands satisfying associations in which he can feel secure and accepted and in which he can reveal himself."[5] Man discovers his identity in community; he thinks through the internalizing of the "other's" conversation. He deliberates and decides dialogically. The child interiorizes the demands of social existence in authoritarian forms which are hopefully outgrown. To be human, he must respond within a social context and accept accountability for his actions. Of course all these social contexts are sinful. Of course man shrinks from the call to responsibility (responsibility to a center of value and for fellowman). Of course, as Ebeling explains, man cannot ultimately render account for himself. Yet there is a basic goodness and necessity in the ego-alter dialectic which prompts our contention that conscience is fallen in man but that man is not conscientious because he is fallen. He is conscientious because he is social, political, and teleological, and to quote Genesis, all of these are "very good."

In conscience, man is called to responsibility. The community-in-the-self summons the self to integrity in community under the transcendent values or purposes of the community. The unique self is addressed and called to true manhood. He is called in freedom to find identity and integrity in relationship. The call is to a unity of integrity and responsibility, to a unity of the self and its neighbors in the God in whom both live and move. The problem is that this call comes from "a people of unclean lips" and when the self responds it is as "a man of unclean lips." Man in his sinful self-assertion and self-desertion flees responsibility and follows graceless gods up blind alleys.

Judgment: Conscience and Responsibility in Cleavage

In the anxiety of his creaturehood and in distrust of the power which has thrust him into existence, man chooses the way of *self-defined unity* as the justification of his existence and finds that way ending in *self-confined disunity.* He thinks goodness is to be acquired as a status instead of accepted as a covenant. The attempt is made to assume responsibility for the self in isolation from or manipulation of God and neighbor or to evade all responsibility. Integrity shrinks to a selfish pre-occupation instead of being a social realization of the responsible life. The gaze focuses not on divine will and human need but on how I can be good and constitute my own existence by being my own judge and jury. Conscience then does not summon to responsibility; it either rationalizes an irresponsibility for the sake of self-righteousness or attacks irresponsibility without offering forgiveness.

One way sinful conscience is experienced is in terms of disunion or disintegration. When a being created to be a social self under a transcendent sovereign attempts to be a separately secure and sovereign self, the absence of the external bands results in an internal "coming unglued." Bonhoeffer distinguishes shame, which testifies to disunion with God and neighbor, from conscience, which testifies to disunion with the self, but for our purposes the two are inseparable.[6]

This inner cleavage which reflects alienation in relationships is experienced in various forms. St. Paul describes the agonized conscience when he writes to the Romans (chapter 7) about the gap between what we know to do and what we actually do. He did not understand his actions. Thielicke speaks of a split between good and evil polarities of the self in which conscience alternately accuses and defends in a conflict between two warring parties in the person.[7] Paul Lehmann describes an inner division when he writes, "The paradox is that *we do not know the will of God which we will and we do not will the will of God which we know.*"[8]

Sometimes the cleavage makes itself felt in one's guilt over an act which does not fit one's ideal self-image. Frank Alpine, the Assistant in Bernard Malamud's novel by that title, experienced that agony of spirit after he had raped the girl he loved:

> He lay in bed with the blankets pulled over his head, trying to smother his thoughts but they escaped and stank. The more he smothered them the more they stank. He smelled garbage in the bed and couldn't move out of it. He couldn't because he was it—the stink in his own broken nose. What you did was how bad you smelled. Unable to stand it he flung the covers aside and struggled to dress but couldn't make it. The sight of his bare feet utterly disgusted him. He thirsted for a cigarette but couldn't light one for fear of seeing his hand. He shut his eyes and lit a match. The match burned his nose. He stepped on the lit match with his bare feet and danced to pain.
>
> O my God, why did I do it? Why did I ever do it? Why did I do it?
>
> His thoughts were killing him. He couldn't stand them. He sat on the edge of the twisted bed, his thoughtful head ready to burst in his hands. He wanted to run. Part of him was already in flight, he didn't know where. He just wanted to run. But while he was running he wanted to be back. He wanted to be back with Helen, to be forgiven. It wasn't asking too much. People forgave—who else?[9]

Bonhoeffer calls this sorrow over transgressions "remorse" and distinguishes it from "shame," a more generalized sense of loss of unity, but both are facets of uneasy conscience.[10] As Bonhoeffer's description of shame suggests, often the feeling of disintegration and the desire to be at one is not focused on particular acts but merely expresses a general unease. Celia says to the psychiatrist, Reilly, in T. S. Eliot's *The Cocktail Party:*

> It's not the feeling of anything I've ever *done*,
> Which I might get away from, or of anything in me
> I could get rid of—but of emptiness, of failure
> Towards someone, or something, outside of myself;
> And I feel I must ... *atone*—is that the word?
> Can you treat a patient for such a state of mind?[11]

Celia had not been brought up to believe in sin "in the usual sense." Anything wrong was either "bad form" or psychological. Yet she felt estranged. Celia's inner division is not connected to a specific act as Frank's is, but it is the outgrowth of a relationship with a man in which they were only using each other and were actually strangers, capable of neither giving nor receiving love.

The division of conscience which separates integrity and responsibility is experienced with respect to the laws of social life. Whereas these should guide the life of the human community, they become barriers between the self and God and between the self and the neighbor. They are alien because the source of life is seen as enemy. The conscience that should be man's bond with God and man becomes barrier against God and neighbor, due to the belief that God is against the self or that some other god is Savior and Lord of the self. The moral dictates of conscience in sin may be much the same as the content in salvation, but there is an essential distinction. The object of accountability of the conscience is either not the same, or the relation to it is infinitely different. In fear and hostility, the demands of corporate life are obeyed. Civilization is continued, but communion is confounded. Sin is restrained, but not resolved. Social sanctions are internalized as self-punishment instead of appropriated as avenues to self-realization.

Division is also experienced in our feeling that we are many people rather than one because we serve many communities and causes without finding a consistent identity or establishing value priorities. The self is "all things to all men"— not in the sense of universal responsibility and neighbor-centeredness but in the sense of "spreading oneself too thin" and of "other-directedness." The conscience thus "goes to pieces." In its polytheism it responds to everything but the One that can give wholeness.

The plight of conscience in its divided eccentricity is captured well in some lines the father speaks in *Six Characters in Search of an Author* by Luigi Pirandello:

> For the drama lies all in this—in the conscience that I have, that each of us has. We believe this conscience to be

a single thing, but it is many-sided. There is one for this person and one for that. Diverse consciences. So we have this illusion of being one person for all, of having a personality that is unique in all our acts. But it isn't true. We perceive this when, tragically perhaps, in something we do, we are as it were, suspended, caught up in the air by a kind of hook. Then we perceive that all of us was not in that act, and that it would be an atrocious injustice to judge us by that action alone, as if all our existence were summed up in that one deed.[12]

In proclaiming that Jesus did sum up all his existence in one deed, the Christian recognizes that as sinner he is unable thus to "pull himself together." We humpty-dumpties have had a great fall, and in our disunity and our search for integrity we often come to admit that "all the king's horses and all the king's men" couldn't put us together again, despite our efforts to put things right and answer for ourselves. We are each "six characters in search of an author."

If this admission comes at all, however, it does not come before we have had a try or two at making things right ourselves. We settle for our little legalisms and kid ourselves into thinking we have bridged the gulf between "the ethical claim and the ethical act," to use Lehmann's phrase. We make "morality," rather than love, our aim. We attempt to be good for our own sake instead of for others' sakes. We anesthetize or busy ourselves to keep from facing ourselves. To make a name for ourselves we drop names to get glory by association and call names to get elevation through degradation. We judge people to feel superior and flee from judging issues for fear that we might be mistaken. This sinful conscience may be either blunted and deceptively silent or loudly condemnatory, but it is bad conscience whether it is sensitive or insensitive. Niebuhr contrasts in these words either form of bad conscience with the conscience that is reconciled and thus good:

> The choice does not lie between the good conscience of a self which has kept all its laws and the bad conscience of the transgressor, but between the dull conscience which does not discern the greatness of the other and the loftiness of his demands, the agonized conscience of the awakened, and the consoled conscience of one who in the com-

pany of the spirit seeks to fulfill the infinite demands of the infinite other.[13]

Conscience reflects the consequences of sin not only in the judgment resident in sundered selfhood, but also in its adoption of false alter-egos. In the case of Eichmann, a more fundamental manifestation of sin than his failure to measure up to his community's standard was his allegiance to the Nazi community and its god. Not only does polytheism or polydemonism divide the self, but identification with perverse societies and sinister or second-rate centers of value enslaves the self. Man's idolatry pulls him apart toward many gods, many social systems, many emotional sovereignties; it also pulls him together around false messiahs and locks him in closed societies. In either case, the one ultimate power and source of ultimate meaning which is God is either not responded to at all or is responded to in fear and hostility, as enemy, not as friend, to borrow from H. Richard Niebuhr. Alienation and idolatry are twin approaches to the estrangement of sinful man from himself, his neighbor, and the living God, and also to the divisions within and among communities which are in turn reflected in individual selves.

Catholic approaches to the effect of sin on conscience usually assess the ravages of fallenness less radically. What is wrong with conscience is more a lack than a loss. It is more attributable to a confusion in man's knowledge of the good than to a "cussedness" which rebels against the good it knows. Bernhard Häring emphasizes the need of grace due to the effects of sin on man's affinity for and knowledge of the good, but his position still tends toward the idea that conscience without Christ is more neutral than negative. He compares conscience without Christ to a candle without a flame and to a voice with no words of its own.[14] The idea is more one of a container that needs filling than of a disposition that needs a turnabout, or a cleavage which must be healed. Divine law specifies and clarifies the natural law which conscience does know.

It is in reaction to Catholic views of conscience as the point of contact for revelation, as receiver for it, as judge of its credibility, that Protestant writers such as Lehmann, Bonhoeffer, and Thielicke take underestimates of the radicality of evil to task and view all "point of contact" talk with deep suspicion. They point to conscience's placing of barriers in the way of hearing the gospel. Against suggestions that man's rationality is indestructible, Thielicke for instance rejoins that reason is "a free and dangerous vagabond"[15] unless it has a foundation. The *imago dei* must be seen as relational rather than resident in man. Thielicke airs his emphasis on the antithesis between conscience under law and conscience in the gospel and the limited usefulness of "point of contact" talk in these words:

> ... the "old" conscience and the "new" cannot be brought together under the common rubric "conscience," as something which in form remains a constant factor, indifferent in respect to the contents which may fill it from time to time. The reference here is not to two stages in the history of the one conscience but to a total destruction of the old and a wholly fresh structuring of the new. Both take place in the miracle of the Holy Spirit, which is why we can know nothing of "how" this break takes place. This is also why we can speak of "contact" only in a derived sense, since the term secretly implies this whole problem of "how" it all takes place. "Point of contact" is a borderline concept, a figure of speech to help our understanding; we use it only in the way a school teacher uses chalk on the blackboard, to make a point and then to rub out immediately what he has written.[16]

He calls the agonized conscience "the no-man's-land" between law and gospel, between conscience as defense against God and God as defense against conscience.[17]

"Point of contact" may be a borderline concept, but unless, with Karl Barth, we are to take the position that the Holy Spirit makes man's response to the gospel wholly for him and unless we are to say that the gospel replaces conscience rather than converts it, we must not erase the concept as quickly as Thielicke does. If *conscience* points to man's questionableness (Ebeling), his addressability, his ego-alter dialogue, and if man does respond to the gospel because it somehow "speaks to him," then conscience *is* the place of contact. Leslie Dewart, in his book *The Future of Belief,* has suggested that our experience of presence to ourselves which includes an experience of transcendence may be the best avenue we have for conceiving of God. Since our own experience of presence to ourselves is an insufficient explanation of the presence that enables us to know ourselves, and thus to transcend ourselves, we are pointed beyond ourselves to a Presence which is the source of true self-knowledge.[18] This can be tied to Ebeling's designation of conscience as "hermeneutical principle."

The shift from despair to deliverance, from agony to ecstasy, from experience of questionableness to being answered for, from experience of presence to experience of God is not an inevitable one. Man rejects the love he seeks and continues to listen to the voices of false gods, but conscience as a reminder of lost integrity and as disposition toward the self's supreme good and as the place of meeting between the self and the community is fulfilled as well as called into question by the good news.

Redemption: Conscience as Responsibility

Good conscience does not come about through more fresh starts and greater moral exertion and an extra boost from an intake of grace to get us over the hump. Man cannot bridge the gap between what is and what ought to be. Good conscience comes with the faith which turns the sovereignty of the self over to God, which believes that the Ultimate Other with whom we have to deal is friend as well as judge, and which finds wholeness within and reconciliation with neighbor through union with God. Salvation is reconciliation of the alienated to communion; it is deliverance from the necessity of answering for oneself to the possibility of grateful response to a Word which is answer and summons, permission and demand. Faith trusts that God really is for us and not against us, that his judgment is the chastisement of his love. It is in Jesus Christ that the Christian believes this reconciliation has "come through" to him.

Richard Niebuhr has incisively suggested that *reconciliation* is a more adequate and inclusive motif for the understanding of salvation than those which have characterized the deontologists (justification) and teleologists (restoration of vision or healing of diseased powers). In confessing that we learn God is friend and not enemy in Jesus Christ, he writes: "Through Jesus Christ, through his life, death, resurrection, and reign in power, we have been led and are being led to *metanoia,* to the reinterpretation of all our interpretations of life and death."[19] *Metanoia* brings change from distrust to trust, from fear to faith, from disintegration to wholeness, from eccentric centers of value to God, from ethics of death to ethics of life. The conscience is consoled; it convicts and commands in the context of love. God's wrath and God's love are seen unitively rather than dualistically in Lutheran fashion. The many now can be seen in light of the ultimate One, partial communities in light of universal community, time in the light of the open future of eternity. Distrust remains because the *metanoia* is not complete, but it has been overcome. Now the Christian views life, death, God, neighbor, everything through the symbolic form of Christ.[20]

Niebuhr affirms that under the rubric of responsibility, Jesus Christ acts in two directions. "In him man is directed toward God; in him also God is directed toward men."[21] He makes possible what is impossible for man, his redemption to responsible being. He inaugurates and maintains "the movement beyond resignation to reconciliation."[22] In Niebuhr's words, the Christian confesses:

> . . . we were blind in our distrust of being, now we begin to see; we were aliens and alienated in a strange, empty world, now we begin sometimes to feel at home; we were in love with ourselves and all our little cities, now we are falling in love, we think, with being itself, with the city of God, the universal community of which God is the source and governor. And for all this we are indebted to Jesus Christ, in our history, and in that depth of the spirit in which we grope with our theologies and theories of symbols.[23]

Jesus Christ is not only the revelation of this reconciliation; his Spirit is also its enabler and empowerer. In reconciliations the dialogue in the self has Christ or the Holy Spirit as party to the joint authorship of condemnation, constraint, or call to universal responsibility. As Niebuhr puts it, "when the other in the self, the Holy Spirit, let us say, is loyal to his cause, the universal community, and in light of that cause requires the self to judge itself to be a transgressor, he can yet be friendly to the self."[24] In this life "in Christ" or "in the Spirit," consolation replaces exclusion, and inspiration to fulfill the will of God replaces despair over failure to do so.

This good conscience, which is reconciled to God and to neighbor by the power of divine love, is far more than the absence of a guilty conscience. In fact, the conscience of the forgiven sinner can be good and guilty at once. It finds its personal integrity in responsibility to God for others even to the point of acceptance of guilt. Ultimately guilt is felt in the violation of covenant or betrayal of trust. Conscience then can be friend of responsibility rather than foe.

In the context of reconciliation, awareness of guilt and sensitivity to the demands of love are deepened because the reconciled sinner is free to face himself in his repeated failures to be responsible, but also free from bondage in the circle of self for service and sharing and outgoing concern. The fulcrum of moral selfhood is theocentric, not egocentric. The self has been recentered. Good conscience involves integration in universal community, not just integration of personality. The aim of the self is not "being good," but being good for someone. Conscience for Christ was not a barrier to responsibility, but ultimately a call to accept responsibility. His trust in and loyalty to his Father freed him to accept guilt for others, as Bonhoeffer stressed. In him conscience and covenant were one.

Because the Christian remains both justified and a sinner, he encounters the law of his being (whether externally from community or written on his heart) both as bane and as blessing. He acts out of fear as well as out of love. The voice

of conscience is heard at times as enemy rather than as friend.
He allows his restricted societies to impose their idolatries. He
elevates other self-images beside the one which has been revealed
in Christ, the image of God. He mistakes the voices of the gods
for that of God. He is not always mono-conscientious, because
he is not always monotheistic, and even when he is mono-
conscientious, the voice of conscience may be that of an idol.
Even in good conscience, personality is not a static unity, but
a dynamic dialogue, without which thought and decision and
responsible action would be impossible. Conflict is inevitable
and necessary. In the inner dialogue of selfhood, there continues to be a battle of voices. The temptation of Christ is
illustrative of such battles. Man is not free if he has no alternative. Therefore, the good conscience, from a Christian perspective, is one which knows with itself that "there is none
good but God," which knows where the priorities lie, and
which, amid the thunder of the throng, hears the still, small
voice, speaking for brothers and for a self-image whose calls
would otherwise be drowned out in the din.

6 Conscience, Christ, and Koinonia

He [the Christian] needs a Christian identity, to be sure, and the source of this identity should be none other than Christ. But what does it mean to "identify" with Christ in an urban setting, "to put on Christ" in the city?

. . . .

As an urban people there is hardly anything in the setting of our lives which finds a ready parallel in the setting of Christ's life; physically, culturally, psychologically, it is totally different. Given these dissimilarities, there is only one possible conclusion. It is a basic mistake for a person living today to choose Christ as his concrete identity model. If we take seriously Christ's humanity, then we have to take with equal seriousness his human uniqueness and individuality. He was *not* like us. He was only like himself, just as each of us, once we pare away superficial resemblances, is like no one else.

. . . .

. . . the major significance of Christ for us is that he lived, he died, and he lives still, and that in his words and in a few symbolic actions He left us a guide. If it is Christ who should animate our inner life, who should live within us, in no sense can this animation take the place of our own attempts to form our own identity.

For this latter task there are no patterns. We each have to create our own, and nowhere more than in a fragmented urban society which throws up before its inhabitants few fixed slots, few settled folk-ways, few assurances about either the present or the future. There is no such thing as a ready-made Christian self-identity in an urban society. It is not hidden in Scripture or tradition or history.[1]

The responsible self we see in Christ and which we believe is being elicited in all our race is a universally and eternally responsive I, answering in universal society and in time without end, in all actions upon it, to the action of the One who heals all our diseases, forgives all our iniq-

uities, saves our lives from destruction, and crowns us
with everlasting mercy. The action we see in such life is
obedient to law, but goes beyond all laws; it is form-giving
but even more form-receiving; it is fitting action. It is action which is fitted into the context of universal, eternal,
life-giving acting by the One. It is infinitely responsible in
an infinite universe to the hidden yet manifest principle
of its being and its salvation.[2]

The faith out of which new directions or conscience or
virtues flow comes into being and is nourished by common life in the church . . . This means that the church has
a function in the formation of the person—his mind and
attitudes—as a community moral nurture and discourse
that seeks to relate the legacy of the faith to the life of the
world.[3]

Thus far Jesus Christ has been spoken of primarily either
as Lord of conscience or as the supreme act of God's grace in
enabling the conversion of conscience. For the Christian though,
Christ is not only king and redeemer but also model. In Thielicke's words, "I must first be in a right relation to Christ in
his quality as exemplar before I can follow him as example.
I must first be set in the sun before I can become warm. I must
first know that I am loved before I can love in return."[4] We
do not attain salvation by imitation but by God's action, of
which Christ is the "original prototype," and our response, of
which Christ is also the "original prototype."[5] Salvation produces imitations, not vice versa. However, Jesus Christ is a
model of moral selfhood. The question is, "In what way is
he a model?" Certainly the "Be single, sandled, and sinless"
answer is dead. Bernhard Häring, whose tradition has been
the strongest advocate of *imitatio Christi,* emphasizes that this
imitation means following Christ, not in the manner of "mere
copying of His acts" or "mechanical fulfillment of His words
and law," but living in him and through him and with him.[6]

Imitation and Imagination

The woodenness of a view of following Jesus which inter-
prets imitation to mean doing what he did becomes apparent

in zealous quests for Christ-figures in works of literature which become fixated on external marks. A man with the initials J. C. who meets a violent end in his early thirties is seized upon (i.e., Joe Christmas in Faulkner's *Light in August*) and a woman with only one initial who grows old and endures is often overlooked (i.e., Dilsey in Faulkner's *The Sound and the Fury*). What can happen is that the person has so many characteristics that he has no character, no unique personhood (i.e., Billy Budd, Melville's Christ-figure). As Sallie TeSelle explains so ably in *Literature and the Christian Life*, " . . . Thus, content of imitation is not a repetition of the sequence of events in his life, but a putting on of the mind of Christ, summarized in the Great Commandment."[7] Just as a fictional character's greatness is not in his being "true to type" but in his uniqueness and in the appropriateness of his acts to his identity, the lives of both Christ and the Christian are eviscerated if they become timeless embodiments of great ideas rather than situational centers of action in a historical drama. What TeSelle calls "the unsubstitutable uniqueness of the man Jesus"[8] and of every man is at issue here. Is the Christian called to be another Jesus or to be a follower of Jesus in response as a particular person in his own time and place?

TeSelle aptly seconds Eduard Schweizer's interpretation of following Jesus in making her case for "discipleship" rather than "imitation."[9] Schweizer delineates two senses of "following" in Judaism. One meaning suggested the imitation of the virtues of God; the second referred to the concrete following by a servant of his lord. Schweizer gives ample reason to believe that the Synoptics had the second understanding of following Jesus,[10] and the New Testament as a whole supports this interpretation. Our insistence on the uniqueness of each person should not be taken to mean that discipleship is simply a matter of everyone's "doing his own thing." The life of a person who has the "mind of Christ" or lives "with Christ" or "in Christ" does take on a recognizable configuration—one of total trust in God and of ministering love to others. To quote Professor TeSelle, " . . . the total and persuasive trust in God and love to fellows—receive their concrete contours from the words, acts, and stories of Jesus because . . . he is the one in whom God is present in the world for the salvation of all men."[11] The Christian life is not a shapeless blob; it has a style which is illustrated in the Gospels—a style which still must be tailored to be fitting for the concrete person in his setting. What C. H. Dodd designates as "the *quality* and the *direction*"[12] of the Christian life is set forth without dictation to copy external qualities or issuance of detailed directives.

Man did not have to become the modern urbanite for the lockstep likeness to be a misguided interpretation of discipleship. Jesus called those of his own time not to be him, but to be themselves as God intended. Each person had a unique role to play in the Kingdom of God. The dedicated proponents of "doing what Jesus would do" have usually pretended more than they practiced because their versions of Jesus as the monk, the moral teacher, the "man in the gray flannel suit," the existentialist, or the picket have said more about themselves and their milieu than about the man from Nazareth. As Amos Wilder contends, " . . . in every decade men instruct Christ as to what he was and is instead of allowing themselves to be instructed by him."[13] Michael Harrington has written in his article "Christ as a Hipster,"

> In the 1920's, there was a famous book which pictured Jesus Christ as a businessman. It has been remembered primarily as a symbol of theological Babbitry in those not so dead, dead days when one could confuse the Son of Man with the National Association of Manufacturers.
> Today, the Supreme Being is getting a new image. On picket lines, campuses and even in nightclubs it is rumored that He is a New Leftist, a member of Timothy Leary's psychedelic League for Spiritual Discovery or perhaps even a dues payer to the San Francisco chapter of the League for Sexual Freedom. Yet, this notion of a swinging Deity is, I submit, as essentially manipulative as the Twenties version of Him as the Great Salesman in the Sky. And even though some of my best friends are hip ministers, rabbis and priests, I want to propose (from the outside looking in, to be sure) the very radical thought that there is a place for God . . . in the Church.[14]

What is being described here is manipulation of Christ rather than emulation. This kind of idolatry is often unconscious, but the rationalizations involved are not thereby rendered innocuous. In this regard Wilder observes, "There is, indeed, a sense in which every significant portrayal of Christ must be a modernization. The 'distance' between Nazareth and Detroit, between the first century and the twentieth, must be bridged. But re-portrayal should not be betrayal."[15]

What then are we to do with Jesus? Callahan's suggestion is that, "as urban men, we should take from him that which we need and can use."[16] He immediately realizes that this tack could be taken to mean that one could pick and choose among Jesus' attributes insofar as it suited the purposes of the picker. This is not his intention. He indicates more specifically what the modern man might use:

> His scorn for the law that kills, which we need to have to keep sub-communal mores from stifling the life of the spirit and the laws of the state from becoming an instrument of suppression. His willingness to associate with all men, sinners and saints, harlots and tax collectors, which we need to remind us that every group in the city counts, the rich, the poor, shop-keepers and bureaucrats. His compassion, which we need when we deal with the criminal and the conman, the crowd which runs amok, the policeman who beats the Negro, and the Negro who has been beaten. His eschatological vision, which we need to remind us that the hour is late, that we must begin now building the Kingdom.[17]

But what if we are not as much "where the action is" as Callahan is? What if we are concerned about standards and structures as well as situation and see more of family, office force, and the PTA than we do of the "night people"? Callahan's suggestions are valid, but hardly inclusive, and even if he had extended his list for pages he could not have exhausted the opportunities and responsibilities of the Christian life. How can Christ be a pattern without being a prescription?

The emergent model of Jesus Christ is that of a model of responsible selfhood. In one of the quotations which heads this chapter, H. Richard Niebuhr describes him as the responsible man *par excellence* who made the fitting response, seeing all actions upon him as signs of divine action and looking to infinite response to his actions. Jesus then is the paradigm of responsible life, not in his doing deeds to copy mechanically, but in his interpretation of life. His conscience—responding to God in all actions on him and responsible for universal community—his faith, which is good conscience, is the model. The pattern then is more relational than substantive. In his relation to God and to all his fellowmen, he manifests the image of God which is the reflection of relationship rather than the possession of attributes.[18]

Bonhoeffer's version of Christ as model of responsibility is set within the context of his definition of ethics as "formation." Jesus Christ is "the one form which has overcome the world," and "formation comes by being drawn into the form of Jesus Christ."[19] It is not by trying to be like Jesus that such formation takes place, but through molding by Jesus Christ. The conformity is not to an ideal type, or definite picture of human nature. "The real man is at liberty to be his Creator's creature. To be conformed with the Incarnate is to have the right to be the man one really is."[20] The emphasis is on the specific man in the concrete place where he is, on a concreteness which is quite different from abstract, once-and-for-all ethical theories of the good. This variation of "the here and the now" for each person might suggest total relativism, but Bonhoeffer counters this danger by recourse to the conditioning of one's context, which in the West at least has been strongly influenced by the form of Christ. As he expresses it,

> What prevents this is the fact that by our history we are set objectively in a definite nexus of experiences, responsibilities and decisions from which we cannot free ourselves again except by an abstraction . . . this nexus is characterized in a quite peculiar manner by the fact that until our own days its . . . basis has been the form of Christ.[21]

In summary, "Ethics as formation, then, means the bold endeavour to speak about the way in which the form of Jesus Christ takes form in our world, in a manner which is neither

abstract nor casuistic, neither programmatic nor purely specu-
lative."[22]

The responsible selfhood of Jesus Christ is described by
Bonhoeffer in terms of deputyship. A deputy is one who acts
in the place of others as a father does for a family or a statesman for a nation. "He is not an isolated individual, but he
combines in himself the selves of a number of human beings.
Any attempt to live as though he were alone is a denial of the
actual fact of his responsibility."[23] Jesus lived a life of deputyship for all, and through him all human life becomes essentially
a life of deputyship. All Jesus did was deputyship, and in this
sense Christians are all called, as Luther emphasized, to be
Christs to the neighbor. Of Christ, Bonhoeffer writes, "In this
real deputyship which constitutes His human existence He is
the responsible person *par excellence.*"[24] Because deputyship is
selfless, Bonhoeffer agrees with Goethe's contention that the
man of action is *without conscience,* since conscience is to the
German martyr centered on personal integrity and one's self-
image. Responsibility or deputyship acts; conscience judges. On
this premise, it would be doubtful that Bonhoeffer would speak
of the conscience of Christ, which to this writer reveals a flaw
in Bonhoeffer's argument.

Responsible action in deputyship inevitably becomes guilty
action as we saw earlier. Because Christ was concerned for man's
reconciliation and not for his own goodness, he took guilt
upon himself for man's justification. As justified sinner, the
Christian turns from concern with his own innocence to concern for his neighbor in need.[25] His name should get less and less
in the way of his neighbor. Bonhoeffer's strong and crucial
thrust here is toward the self-forgetfulness of responsibility.
This is a note which must be struck over and over in any treatment of Christ as model or pattern, because one of the dissonant
tones which is forever spoiling such an emphasis is the egocentricity—the spiritual pulse-taking and selfish preoccupation
which have frequently accompanied an ethic centered on the
imitation of Christ. Our quibble with Bonhoeffer is only over
whether one's conscience could not constrain him to responsible
action at the expense of concern for personal rectitude.

Bernhard Häring also fears the linking of an *imitatio* ethic with an ethic of personal salvation or perfection. A person is in a way most responsible for himself since he has most control over himself, but he must not set his worth or value over the Kingdom of God or the salvation of his neighbor. "We cannot," emphasizes Häring, "speak of the imitation of Christ without implying responsibility for every soul redeemed by Christ, without proclaiming responsibility for service in the Kingdom of Christ."[26] His love provides the basis and norm for man's love.

Bonhoeffer defines responsible action not only as action in deputyship, with Jesus Christ as the deputy *par excellence,* but also as action "in correspondence with reality," with Christ as revelation of that reality. In him is the reality which says both the "no" of judgment and the "yes" of redemption to every contingency, and the Christian's action must never say only "yes" or only "no." The Christian is to let men, and with them the world, be what they are in Christ—"loved, condemned and reconciled."[27] Responsible action accords with this reality. Either to separate the Christian and the secular in principle (with the resultant two autonomous realms of pseudo-Lutheranism) or to unite them in principle rather than in Christ (with the resultant mistaking of the world for the Kingdom of God) is to get out of touch with reality.[28]

The strength of this view of Jesus Christ as a paradigm of responsibility is its allowance for the uniqueness of every self's personality and situation along with its provision of an image which is definitive. With this model a person can find his identity without forfeiting his individuality. Here is an image of true humanity which inspires imagination, rather than stifles it. Christ the deputy provides shape and scope for responsibility without imposing straitjacket. Conscience is transformed from a centripetal to a contrifugal force.

Koinonia as Context

One does not have to go the route of John Knox (*The Church and the Reality of Christ*), who submerges Christ from sight in the church, or that of Rudolf Bultmann, who despairs of knowing more than the church's faith concerning Jesus, to believe that the Christian does not know Jesus Christ apart from the church. As the New Testament scholar Roy Harrisville has argued, to be "in Christ" or "in Adam" is to be identified with a community. New birth is wrongly conceived as an individualistic psychological experience. It is finding a new identity in a new community which is the context of conversion and of sanctification.[29]

Daniel Callahan comments that he knows "no major theoreticians working with the idea that the Christian experience may be, at bottom, a social experience"[30] of an aggregate nature as opposed to a one-to-one encounter. He is surely selling short the suggestions found not only in Harrisville, but also in Paul Lehmann and H. Richard Niebuhr.

Bonhoeffer maintains that the church is the point of departure for Christian ethics because Christ is formed in it and his taking form is proclaimed by it. In his words, "Formation ... means in the first place Jesus's taking form in His Church."[31] The church, his body, bears the form which is proper for all men although it is not a model or principle to be superimposed on the whole world.[32] In the church then one learns what true manhood is. It embodies the new humanity.

Paul Lehmann, who, like Bonhoeffer, makes the Christian community the starting point for ethical reflection, describes it as "the *fellowship-creating reality* of Christ's presence in the world."[33] "The ethical reality of the church is the presence in the world of a community within which the achievement of maturity is always both a possibility and a fact."[34] The Christian *koinonia* is both dynamically and dialectically related to the empirical reality of the church since the two are neither identical nor separable. *Koinonia* is the community which enables, embodies, informs new life in Christ. The church as an institution both embodies and belies what it is to be God's people— belies it not because it is an institution, we would contend, but because any specific group of Christians is always but another empirical verification of the doctrine of original sin. It provides the self with an image of man with which it can identify and affords resources for realization of a new self. The *koinonia* defines maturity as "the integrity in and through interrelatedness which makes it possible for each individual member of an organic whole to be himself in togetherness, and in togetherness to be himself."[35]

As Christ is formed in the church and his taking form is proclaimed by it, conscience is also being formed. A perspective is being provided and a style of life is being developed. As Lehmann would express it, conscience is given a context. James Gustafson explains that Lehmann finds Christian behavior coming out of three contexts.[36] The first, largest, and most determinative of these is the context of what God is doing. Faith discerns his humanizing work supremely in Jesus Christ. As Lehmann puts it, "The activity and purposes of God [are] the concrete context from within which behavior can be regarded as both guided and shaped."[37] The third context is provided by the particular situation, the concrete place of Christian activity. What God is doing must be discerned, not by deduction from moral norms, but on the spot. In order to be sensitive to what God in his freedom is doing in the concrete situation to "make and keep human life human" the Christian conscience must be shaped by the Christian community which nurtures a theonomous orientation as well as a situational sensitivity. In this second or *koinonia* context, "ethical theory and practice acquire a framework of meaning and a pattern of action which undergird the diversity and the complexity of the concrete ethical situation with vitality and purpose."[38]

In the *koinonia* man discerns (using both the Bible and the newspaper) and participates in what God is doing in the world. It is a half-truth, Lehmann urges, for Christian ethics to urge man to do the will of God in some generalized sense. The will of God is thus conceived in abstraction from the actual situation and lacks content and relevance.[39] Such admonition fails to take due account of the difficulty of knowing what the will of God is and also of man's sinful unwillingness to do that will of God which he does know. A *koinonia* ethic will be concerned with relations and functions while Lehmann judges that moral theology has been largely absolutistic, exalting ideals, values, and laws as applicable in all situations. But this issue is one which will be saved for the next chapter.

The concern now is to appropriate Lehmann's depiction of *koinonia* as that "which conjoins the focus of divine activity and the focus of human responsiveness in such a way as to provide behavior with direction and decisiveness."[40] Unfortunately Lehmann is loathe to be descriptive of how Christian *koinonia* "tells us how to ascertain the will of God and how we should go about answering ethical questions." Christ is the criterion for discerning the action of God, but Lehmann is so careful not to be prescriptive that he fails to be very descriptive either of the process of decision-making or of a style of life or pattern of response in free obedience to which he refers.[41] Gustafson legitimately complains that Lehmann talks continually about both conscience and *koinonia* but tells the reader much less about either than one would hope.[42]

H. Richard Niebuhr's fourth component of responsibility was, it may be recalled, social solidarity. "Our action," he wrote, "is responsible, it appears, when it is response to action upon us in a continuing discourse or interaction among beings forming a continuing society. A series of responses to disconnected actions guided by disconnected interpretations would scarcely be the action of a self but only of a series of states of mind somehow connected with the same body."[43] Responsible decision then has community context. The differences among men are found in the different societies with which they identify and the differing images of man these societies put forward as representative of the values of the group. The self which is nurtured in a certain family or which finds its identity by integration into a particular community absorbs an ethos.

The actions of both children and adults often reflect the moral riches of an environment which they are not consciously tapping. Certain priorities of concern, certain ways of expressing concern, certain ways of viewing and relating to people are engendered. For instance, whether a person operates under the assumption that, as William Lee Miller put it, "people 'deserve' more than they deserve"[44] rather than under the contention that no one should get anything for nothing may not be an individual decision so much as it is a social pattern. John Gardner elaborates this significance of the influence of ethos:

> Young people do not assimilate the values of their group by learning the words (truth, justice, etc.) and their definitions. They learn attitudes, habits and ways of judging. They learn these in intensely personal transactions with their immediate family or associates. They learn them in the routines and crises of living, but they also learn them through songs, stories, drama and games. They do not learn ethical principles; they emulate ethical (or unethical) people. They do not analyze or list the attributes they wish to develop; they identify with people who seem to them to have these attributes. That is why young people need models, both in their imaginative life and in their environment, models of what man at his best can be.[45]

In the manner Gardner describes, the Christian *koinonia* gives a feel for the appropriate. It shapes a self which reacts almost instinctively to certain obligations while it also furnishes tools for rational discussion and deduction. For the Christian the consistency and continuity for interpretation of action upon the self and for acceptance of accountability for expected responses to its responses is furnished by the church—that community of interaction which centers its loyalty in God, shares the history which centers in Christ, and includes all being in its concern.[46]

Identity and the Intimate Community

The nature of nurture in community context underlines the importance of the more intimate communities which are undermined intentionally by a totalitarian collectivism and inadvertently by the secular city. On every hand we are reminded of the identity crisis of contemporary man. If, as our social understanding of selfhood holds, one discovers who he is only in community, what happens to his self-knowledge when the settled societies of pre-urban man are thrown into their present state of upheaval? The anonymity of the city can give one the freedom to be himself, but it can also prevent him from discovering who he is and from becoming who he can become. It can lead to amnesia as well as to emancipation. The natural communities have suffered dissolution and displacement, and the belongingness and self-identity which go with a well defined social world have often been lost in the process. As a member of many communities a person is concerned about how he is regarded by many reference groups, to use a sociologist's designation. The integrity of the contemporary individual is threatened by an anxiety-producing fragmentation.[47]

The breakdown of the natural communities of kinship, race, color, nationality in which people have formulated an identity can be a healthy development, a release from bondage. For instance, the racial communities of our society gave identity, but it was a case of mistaken identity. The white man's self-understanding was gained at the black man's expense, and the black man's self-understanding was perceived as through the white man's eyes. Both need a new inclusive community in which they can find themselves. They need a larger loyalty to be free for.

Daniel Callahan warns well concerning the need for some close community if self-discovery is to occur:

> [I]f it is true [as psychoanalytic thought affirms] that identity formation requires roots, traditions, models, and goals, then the city as it is taking shape has less and less to offer as a nurturing milieu. . . . In our quest for a totally embracing community of the city we cannot afford to neglect the creation of those smaller communities . . . where the young can work out some sense of who they are, where the old can find friendship and support, and where the sick and the disadvantaged are not left wholly to the mercies of bureaucracy. People don't just live in a city. They live in a particular neighborhood on a particular street surrounded by particular neighbors. That is the city the child knows, his world, his context. Whatever self-identity he forms will, in great part, be formed out of that world and in that context. If we no longer need ghettos

for the assimilation of immigrants, we nonetheless still
need in neighborhoods many of the assets of the ghetto:
common bonds based on real and not fabricated human
needs; a sense of boundary whereby one "little" world can
be distinguished from another; a manageable social structure in which roles can be developed, healthy leadership
take shape, and tradition be established. . . .

. . . .

From the finite, the bounded, the tightly-knit community
a person can work his way *to* the broader community. He
cannot, without running the risk of a total loss of self-
identity, start *from* the broader community. If nothing
else, broader communities rarely exist. They are only
ideals, legal constructs, or sociological generalizations.[48]

The hippy communities and the quest for self-discovery by way
of mind-expanding drugs "trips" illustrate this need which has
been frustrated. The groping will go on for bread which satisfies and for a circle in which to break it.

Callahan's concern for the identity crisis of the young and
the need for neighborhood nurture is paralleled at another
level by the previously-mentioned proposal of Walter Lippmann that the universities must fill a void as a context for
culture formation and guidance in today's world. "Since the
prevailing tradition rests on the prevailing science, it follows
that modern men must look to the company of scholars in the
universities to guard and preserve, to refine and enrich the
tradition of civility."[49] He is concerned that knowledge be trans-
muted into wisdom, which he defines as "soundness of judgment in choice of means and ends."[50] If education is to perform
its primary task, that of instructing future national leaders,
Lippmann asserts that "a body of wisdom must be developed
and communicated—a science which presents the history and
the practice of judging rightly in a choice of means and ends."[51]
Lippmann's rationalism is showing here. He has an overblown
confidence in the ability of the academic community in open-
minded exploration to come up with canons of civility which
could stabilize the ship of state. It is worth a try, though.

Our concern, however, is for conscience formation which is

inclusive of more people than the future leaders of the state
and of more of life than the choice of means and ends for the
good life in society. Likewise our concern extends beyond the
discovery of identity to the recovery of community and the
transformation of society. Are neighborhood togetherness and
academic effort at political casuistry enough? There is evidence
in widespread student protest against the impersonality of education that the basic lack they feel is the lack of community.
As Thomas Langford[52] has observed, the student calls for personal education are rooted in a feeling of isolation which has
not been resolved in his contacts with family and other groups
in society, including the church. He comes to the university
with the fervent hope that he will find community. "Reaching
out with desperation to grasp someone, to meet someone, to be
encountered by someone he can respect, the student turns to
the university and to the teacher. He turns to the university as
the last sanctuary of personal regard and respect. He turns to
the teacher because the teacher is supposed to know—if anyone
does—the fact of human isolation; in addition, he is supposed
to care about his students."[53] When the last hope for a redemptive community, for love is frustrated, as it often is, isolation weighs even heavier and anger often results. The same
dearth of interpersonal relations which the student had experienced before is found at the university. There are recognized
and unrecognized redemptive relationships, but they are all too
few and never plentiful enough to go around.

    When they occur there is often a vertical dimension in-
volved. According to Paul Goodman, "In our impersonal educational establishments, the religious advisor may be the one
responsive person with whom human concerns can be discussed."[54] This locus of the personal may indicate that merely
human relationships are being accorded a faith that is sure to
be frustrated. Langford suggests that, for the Christian community "to witness to the primacy of man's relation to God is
to lift a burden from human relationships which they cannot
carry. It is to free friendship from the effort to be more than it
can possibly be; it is to let human interaction be human—and

relaxed; it is to forego the requirement that partial reality be ultimate."[55] Paul Goodman believes that despite his preservation of the personal the chaplain cannot revive the dead Western tradition and has no doctrine to teach.[56] Some of us would contend that if the chaplain is at times bearing witness in the way Goodman admits, he is communicating something of substance which is at the heart of the Judeo-Christian tradition and which has some connection with such an ancient doctrine as justification by grace through faith.

Paul Goodman is not the only extra-ecclesiastical apologist for the church's mission one could cite. Nor is the university the only arena where the church may be the bearer of redemptive resources. We find Milton Kotler of the Institute for Policy Studies in Washington, D.C., saying that "the church is the only institution with the ideas, motivation and resources to restore real community to the neglected slums of inner-city America."[57] "Churchmen," says Kotler, "are the only ones who have both a continuing existential interest in human community plus a fund of images and ideas to draw upon."[58] We have sociologists such as Talcott Parsons insisting on the necessary function of religion as integrator, harmonizer, and provider of society with its highest ideals. Then there is controversial community-organizer Saul Alinsky saying that the labor unions have sold out to the establishment and the churches are the last hope. "The Christian churches are taking the leadership in social change. The church is less compromised than other institutions maybe because it has a gospel that constantly forces it to think about siding with the poor even when this goes against its own institutional interests."[59] From all these men outside the church we have testimony to the transcendent power which has been entrusted to a very earthen vessel.

There are those within the church who concur. Hubert Humphrey insists that there would have been no civil rights bill without the churches. Daniel Callahan believes that those rare broader communities "can be brought into real existence only by people who know that they need the small religious and neighborhood community but at the same time know that

these microcosms need to be united in a workable and productive and mutually rewarding whole."[60] It might appear that we
are building up a pragmatic argument for church preservation.
Such is not the case. Rather we are merely indicating that the
church can make contributions that the nay-sayers overlook and
that these contributions grow out of ideas, images, motives, resources which are not always remembered when the churchman
joins with other "men of goodwill" in some common social
cause.

Involvement and the Institutional

These appraisals of the church's significance should also
occasion second thoughts about some contemporary reductionistic views of the true mission of the church. How is a person to
find his identity in the church if the Christian community does
not have a distinct identity, a need Callahan urges, and how is
it to maintain an identity and provide a context for conscience
which has some constancy if it is not in some sense an institution?

There are the Brunnerians among us who berate anything
institutional which the Christian community develops as a fall
from the purity of *ekklesia*.[61] Then there are the radical secular-
ists who in their healthy suspicion of the church's institutional
self-centeredness want to see Christians immersed in the institutions, pressure groups, and protest movements of society. In
arising each morning and like a compulsive gambler asking
"where the action is"[62] one discovers the meaning of discipleship. Reacting against the enclave mentality which has characterized the church as an anxious and jealous protector of
conquered territory, these guerrilla fighters attempt to search
out and destroy all the demonic forces which cripple the human
spirit and foster injustice and oppression. In their zeal for the
battlefront, they may forget the training camp. Liturgy may be
left behind in their zeal for legislation. Education may totally
give way to action. The responsibility for the church member
who is not so *avant garde* may be scuttled and the impact of

the Christian faith as a society via the fringe member is overlooked.[63]

James Gustafson's article "A Theology of Christian Community?"[64] raises several telling questions with the radical sec-
ularists who believe their strategy will overcome both the em-
barrassment of the individualistic pietism and the pragmatic
institutionalism in the church and the distance between the
Christian faith and the centers of power which really make the
world go around. He wants to know "whether the division
between the private and the public, the personal and the structural is not too sharply drawn" by the *avant garde* Christians
and "whether significant relations do not exist between them."
From a social psychological perspective he wonders "where the
person-forming communities are going to be in a program of
action that looks with disdain upon the church and other private spheres." Gustafson continues:

> What is to shape the mind and the spirit of the person
> who is told to be completely identified with the "world"?
> What is to provide a center of his own personal existence
> which informs his involvement in the secular order when
> religion, as a historical movement influencing persons and
> cultures, is apparently not to be cultivated? What kind of
> sociological assumptions lie behind the view that Chris-
> tians can be socially more effective by involvement with
> secular institutions, since it is through these that history
> is being shaped, while at the same time the institutions
> and the religious culture that shape the Christians are
> judged to be increasingly useless? Where, also, is the posi-
> tive place of custom and of cultural values, of *ethos*, in
> this critical material? In the anti-bourgeois stance, have
> critics failed to distinguish between false and suppressive
> moral customs and order, on the one hand, and the posi-
> tive significance of cultural morality on the other?[65]

We are reminded of a line in Shaw's *Misalliance* in which the
social bond is compared to a corset. Percival is replying to
Hypatia's suggestion that he wants to do as he likes just as she
does. He insists that he does not. ". . . I tell you I'm not prepared to cast off the social bond. It's like a corset: it's a support

to the figure if it does squeeze and deform it a bit. I want to be free." When Hypatia counters that she is tempting him to be free, he replies, "Not at all. Freedom, my good girl, means being able to count on how other people will behave."[66] The restraints and obligations imposed by community life can be positively valuable for the common good as well as repressive of the individual.

If the church is only a band of compulsive gamblers, where and how are they to be educated and nurtured to know "where the action is"? What provides the context for discerning the demonic and/or angelic elements in that action and for determining how the self can cooperate with God's action in the world? Where will the conscience be shaped which can relate the good news to the daily news if not in a community with a distinct identity which says "but not of the world" as loudly as it does "in the world"? The salt must be purified for resprinkling if relevance is not to turn into betrayal. Undramatic undertakings like the day-to-day existence of the Christian family, the week-to-week deliberations of church study groups, the steadfast structure of congregational life cannot be forgotten in the legitimate concern for social action. One of the songs in *Guys and Dolls* refers to the "oldest, established, permanent floating crap game in New York." Notice that it was *established* as well as *floating*. A will-o'-the-wisp movement is not apt to be sufficiently permanent and powerful to do the job in relation to larger social issues in a bureaucratized, institutionalized society. John Bennett advances a pertinent caveat at this point:

> The widespread rebellion against all institutional forms condemns the church to futility in relation to these larger issues. It also leaves local groups without the support they need from a presbytery or bishop or board. Bureaucracies are necessary to give the church an independent base in relation to each local situation. I have often noticed that some of the most prophetic churchmanship comes out of the bureaucracies, both denominational and ecumenical.
>
> .   .   .   .
>
> Critics of the larger institutional framework tend to kick

away the ladder that enabled them to climb to the point where they can see what they see.[67]

The attacks of the institutional (especially the religiously institutional) may overlook what Michael Novak recognizes: "even the most unrelieved and oppressive of the institutional churches convey (sometimes despite themselves) a sense of history, a sense of community, a sense of mystery."[68] It just may be that Christ's presence and rule can be counted on in the church as much as in social crisis.[69] This faith does not put the institution beyond criticism, but it does remind us that the earthen vessel still has a treasure. Novak's statement suggests by implication that the church will have no identity without memory, community, and mystery, and without an identity it can hardly shape the responsible self. Either the church is a people with a past or it is not the church. Either it is the fellowship of the faithful or it is not the church. Either it worships or it dies. Michael Harrington has said it well.

> The church will not regain its vitality—if that is to happen—by simply being hipper than thou. It must, to be sure, fight for the earthly implications of the heavenly values it affirms; it can never again divorce God from the Negroes, the poor, those dying in war and the rest of humanity. But over and above that witness to the temporal meetings of the eternal, there must be the assertion of the eternal itself. And, amid all the showmanship and swinging theology, that is what I miss.
>
> And so, my radical advice to these radical religionists is: God should go to church. And maybe He shouldn't hang around the bars so much.[70]

Transformation of Selves and Social Structures

Corporate worship and Christian education and small community life are not ready for consignment to the museum or the mortuary yet if the church is going to nurture responsible selves as well as train riot squads. The sad thing is that in the name of preparing persons for Christian living the church has often neglected the relation of the gospel to social issues and the transformation of social structures. And what is more, its attempts at changing individuals have frequently been questionable exercises in conscience formation. Pietism, moralism, and a legalistic obsession with a select group of sins have made morality more a straitjacket than a style of life, more an exercise in self-purification than of social reformation. The persistent dispute in the church over whether its primary mission is the salvation of souls or the reconstruction of society has been a misplaced debate and a grand mistake. Neither is it enough to say that the church should do both. What must be realized is that the conversion of conscience and the conversion of community are inseparable. Work at it from either side and you affect the other side. If social psychology has taught us anything, we should know that man's selfhood does not stop with his skin. The personality is interpenetrated by the societies of the self, and the societies are in turn molded by the members. Dr. Eleanor Haney has expressed it this way: "The transformation of culture is simultaneous with the transformation of the individual. . . . the transformation of one does not seem to occur without the transformation of the other."[71]

One of the most powerful testimonies to the social nature of conscience which Haney's dissertation presents is found in this conclusion about the people who swam against the stream in racial crisis: "One of the outstanding characteristics of those who found it so agonizing to remain consistent was their sense of being alone. Although personal integrity is not simply a microcosm of one's ethos, it does not seem possible apart from close relationship with an ethos."[72]

If conscience is to hear the voice of God, it will hear it in and through that community which discerns God's action in human life, which acknowledges God as ultimate authority, which embodies true community, and which points above itself to the Other who drives it beyond itself to universal responsibility. This Christian community is found in the church, but it is not to be equated with it. Lehmann has rightly cautioned that *koinonia* is both dynamically and dialectically related to the empirical reality of the church, and Bonhoeffer is at pains to distinguish "the communion of the saints" from the empirical church. The church as an institution or organization both embodies and belies what it is to be God's people. It violates as well as preserves Christian community. Like other human societies, it tends to absolutize itself. *Koinonia* or true community is not to be simply identified with the church, but conversely it cannot be separated from it. The church is the earthen vessel in which the treasure has been placed, but the transcendent power belongs not to it, but to God (II Cor. 4:7).

When the church is genuinely the Christian community, it provides the context for the educating of the Christian conscience by pointing to the larger context of God's action, to the whole family of man, and to the whole of being. In Christ, as Bonhoeffer would say, the Christian sees God and the world together. The church's corporate life embodies integrity in Christ, and its mission consists of responsibility to God in the world for the world. In the conscience which the Christian community shapes, this integrity and this responsibility are one. The church properly finds its integrity only in responsibility, and its responsibility reveals the ground of its integrity.

As with any self in any community, the inner dialogue of the self which is part of this community will make for a joint authorship of the voice of conscience. As Niebuhr indicates, the "other" which is represented in the self is the self-in-the-community and the community-in-the-self. What is primarily communicated to the Christian and appropriated by him is thus covenant rather than concept, a relation rather than a prescription, an orientation rather than codification. The Christian education of the self nurtures the person in a whole ethos or characteristic style of life, not just an ethic, narrowly conceived.

The context afforded by the Christian community for conscience does have content, however. It includes the memory and expectation of Jesus, the responsible self whose responses to all actions on him were ultimately responses to God. In the memory and mind-set of this community are the Exodus and the Decalogue, the crucifixion and the resurrection of Jesus, the Sermon on the Mount and Romans 12. The thought and action of this fellowship are informed by generalizations about appropriate behavior for Christians in the form of principles and standards, and Christians reflect on the facts of their situation in light of their commitments and those generalizations in making moral judgments.

The constancies of Christians' responses through the ages make for a continuity among Christian consciences wherever they are found; but when it comes to spelling out the details, there are also as many variations on the common theme or themes as there are Christians. It is not ethical atomism to affirm that unique selves with unique histories and hopes in unique situations appropriate the community's ethos in an individualized way. The experience of the community as it is directly communicated in relationship and as it is recorded in its written accounts of the life of God's people in the past provides guidance, but the guidance cannot preclude the necessity for the responsible self to appropriate and decide, in his own time and place and relationships, what is appropriate response for him. In the next chapter the relation between principles and situation, between obedience and freedom, must be explored.

7 Conscience, Context, and Content

Johnny. You can draw a line and make other chaps toe it. That's what I call morality.
Lord Summerhays. Very true. But you don't make any progress when you're toeing a line.[1]

Jesus stands before God as the one who is both obedient and free. As the obedient one He does His Father's will in blind compliance with the law which is commanded Him, and as the free one He acquiesces in God's will out of His own most personal knowledge, with open eyes and a joyous heart; He re-creates this will, as it were, out of Himself. Obedience without freedom is slavery; freedom without obedience is arbitrary self-will. Obedience restrains freedom; and freedom ennobles obedience. Obedience binds the creature to the Creator, and freedom enables the creature to stand before the Creator as one who is made in His image. Obedience shows man that he must allow himself to be told what is good and what God requires of him (Micah 6.8); and liberty enables him to do good himself. Obedience knows what is good and does it, and freedom dares to act, and abandons to God the judgement of good and evil. Obedience follows blindly and freedom has open eyes. Obedience acts without questioning and freedom asks what is the purpose. Obedience has its hands tied and freedom is creative. In obedience man adheres to the decalogue and in freedom man creates new decalogues (Luther).

In responsibility both obedience and freedom are realized.[2]

What then is *love* and what do we mean by God and by neighbor when we speak of the ultimate purpose of the Church, and so of theological education, as the increase of love of God and neighbor among men? By love we mean at least these attitudes and actions: rejoicing in the presence of the beloved, gratitude, reverence and loyalty toward him. Love is rejoicing over the existence of the beloved one; it is the desire that he be rather than not be;

it is longing for his presence when he is absent; it is happiness in the thought of him; it is profound satisfaction over everything that makes him great and glorious. Love is gratitude: it is thankfulness for the existence of the beloved; it is the happy acceptance of everything that he gives without the jealous feeling that the self ought to be able to do as much; it is a gratitude that does not seek equality; it is wonder over the other's gift of himself in companionship. Love is reverence: it keeps its distance even as it draws near; it does not seek to absorb the other in the self or want to be absorbed by it; it rejoices in the otherness of the other; it desires the beloved to be what he is and does not seek to refashion him into a replica of the self or to make him a means to the self's advancement. As reverence love is and seeks knowledge of the other, not by way of curiosity nor for the sake of gaining power but in rejoicing and in wonder. In all such love there is an element of the "holy fear" which is not a form of flight but rather deep respect for the otherness of the beloved and the profound unwillingness to violate his integrity. Love is loyalty; it is the willingness to let the self be destroyed rather than that the other cease to be; it is the commitment of the self by self-binding will to make the other great. It is loyalty, too, to the other's cause—to his loyalty.[3]

Lord Summerhays' definition of morality above is one which agrees with the conception held by many of the "old morality." Along with the previously mentioned movement toward rejection of authoritarian control and even of any authority at all has gone the questioning of all moral absolutes which draw lines to be unexceptionably toed. The Kantian ethical style of applying universal moral rules to particular moral decisions has come under attack both in theoretical debate and because of practical dilemmas. Kant's oft cited advocation of telling the truth even to the assassin seeking a person hiding in your house serves as an illustration of the straitjacket of a legalism which cannot bend to the situation.

In Christian ethics the context-versus-principles discussion is one which has been lively for several decades. In fact one could begin his tracing of the debate with Jesus versus the Pharisees and Paul versus the Judaizers. However, the problem now presents itself in new and more radical forms. The journalistic writings of John A. T. Robinson, of Joseph Fletcher and others, have triggered widespread popular discussion of and adherence to "the new morality." Although this book is not primarily an addition to the burgeoning literature on "the new morality" debate, a thorough treatment of conscience and responsibility should not by-pass crucial issues which are also central in assessment of "the new morality."

It needs saying at the outset that the context-versus-principles debate has been oversimplified and misplaced, as James Gustafson has pointed out.[4] The lines have been drawn in a misleading fashion. Vastly variant "emphasizers of principles" have been grouped with equally diverse "contextualists." Moreover, as Gustafson states, thorough work in Christian ethics must finally take at least four base points of Christian moral discourse into account, regardless of where the ethicist starts or chooses to place his emphasis. These are: (1) social or situational analysis; (2) fundamental theological affirmations; (3) moral principles; and (4) the nature of the Christian's life in Christ and its appropriate moral expressions in intention and action.[5] Efforts to put all the eggs in one of these baskets are simplistic, and of course attempts to put all the eggs in two of the baskets simultaneously are downright contradictory. Joseph Fletcher says both that the situation should determine moral decision and that love should. As Gustafson points out, Fletcher cannot have it both ways. If love is an absolute, something is brought to the situation, which if it has any shape will shape decision.[6]

Having cautioned that the debate is misplaced, and that "both-and" answers will be sounder than reductionisms of the "either-or" variety, we must still examine the law-liberty issue. We proceed now to review some contributions on both sides of the question and to suggest the relevance of both for a reassessment of conscience.

Freedom and the Situational

Although some non-legalists such as Paul Ramsey, John C. Bennett, and Edward L. Long have emphasized the place and relevance of rules and principles, the current trend is definitely in the direction of greater emphasis on freedom, spontaneity, situational sensitivity, and love as an attitude, and less on law, obligation, ethical constancies, and love as "in-principled," to borrow a term from Paul Ramsey. In the spirit of the times, there is a demand that the traditional in terms of morals be reexamined, and a revolt against submission to restrictions which are not understood or for which no reason is seen. The existentialist emphasis on unfettered freedom, realization of authentic existence, the discontinuity between "moments," and the autonomy of the unique self have been potent forces in the revolt against heteronomy and the reverence for the encounter between the I and the Thou in a unique situation.

This trend has received support in varying ways and degrees from several of the key figures whose views on conscience we have examined. Bonhoeffer has sought to undermine the rule of rules for theological reasons. The will of a God whose action is dynamic and concrete cannot be tied up in a neat package. This will, which is already a reality in God's revelation in Jesus Christ, is "nothing other than the becoming real of the reality of Christ with us and in our world . . . not an idea, still demanding to become real."[7] The responsible self creates the will of God out of himself as he heeds the command of God which comes in the situation and cannot be known in advance.[8] General principles run the risk of reducing the will of God to an abstraction. Bonhoeffer's concern is not with "what is good once and for all, but the way in which Christ takes form among us here and now."[9] Concentration on abstract values, abstract individuals and abstract issues fails to come to grips with the way life is really lived. Since the Christian should be asking "What is the will of God?"—not "How can I be or do good?"[10]—he must seek ever anew to "prove" (Romans 12:2) that will which is "something new and different in each different situation in life."[11] All man's powers—heart, understanding, observation, and experience "all . . . embraced and pervaded by prayer"[12]—must collaborate to know this ever new will. This proving is not done by intuition (although Bonhoeffer has been accused of intuitionism) or by application of a set of rules. On the specific issue of truth telling, Bonhoeffer writes, "If my utterance is to be truthful it must in each case be different according to whom I am addressing, who is questioning me, and what I am speaking about. The truthful word is not in itself constant; it is as much alive as life itself."[13]

James Gustafson speaks for Bonhoeffer as well as himself on this score when he writes:

> The Christian life is lived in obedient response to the living God. Much can be known about his nature and activity, about what he enables and requires men to be or do. But the human response *is not to propositions or knowledge about God;* it is the living God active in creation, in the Son Jesus Christ, and in the Holy Spirit in the Church, to whom the world and the Church in the world are called to obedience. This is response not to a single portrait of Jesus Christ, etched by the imagination, rather to the living Son of the Father, who is risen Lord, teacher, example, redeemer and sanctifier. It is response not to a moral consensus drawn out of Scripture or tradition, but to the promptings of the Holy Spirit as men deliberate together to discern the mind of Christ in their moral responsibilities. An understanding of moral life as related to the living God sits loose to the saddle of all closed rational systems of ethics—Christian or philosophical.[14]

Paul Lehmann makes a similar theological point with his emphasis on the freedom of God's action, and H. Richard Niebuhr does the same with his "radical monotheism."

Bonhoeffer reinforces his position with a distinction between "the ethical" and "the commandment." The former denotes the limited sphere of the prohibited and allowed, which it seems is also the sphere of conscience for Bonhoeffer. Ethical obligation keeps watch on the untransgressable frontiers of life and is far from inclusive of all of life, while the commandment of God, revealed in Jesus Christ, is inclusive. Commandment includes the ethical, but it is permission as well as obligation. Commandment comes in the concrete situation.[15] All decisions are not ethical ones, and to make them so is to fail to confine the ethical phenomenon to its proper place and to deprive man of the freedom which is permitted or commanded by God's

commandment as opposed to all human laws.[16] Marriage illustrates Bonhoeffer's distinction:

> If I love my wife, if I accept marriage as an institution of
> God, then there comes an inner freedom and certainty of
> life and action in marriage; I no longer watch with suspi-
> cion every step that I take; I no longer call in question
> every deed that I perform. The divine prohibition of
> adultery is then no longer the centre around which all my
> thought and action in marriage revolves. (As though the
> meaning and purpose of marriage consisted of nothing
> except the avoidance of adultery!) But it is the honouring
> and the free acceptance of marriage, the leaving behind
> of the prohibition of adultery, which is now the precon-
> dition of the fulfilment of the divine commission [man-
> date] of marriage. The divine commandment has here be-
> come the permission to live in marriage in freedom and
> certainty.[17]

Like Luther, Bonhoeffer is out after the attempt to "be
good." He is concerned that the self shake off the cautious
agonizing which is afraid of making a misstep. Within the limits
of the ethical, a person can live with the nonchalance of faith,
expecting certain knowledge of God's will in the concrete situation, not by direct inspiration, but through a genuine decision,
which itself becomes part of that will. He can cease being
anxious about whether he has done the right thing or not,[18]
because he leaves the judgment to Christ. Ceasing to judge
with the use of the law, he can act in true fulfillment of the
law for the first time. Hearing, he responds.

His responsibility is the totality of his response to the reality
given in Jesus Christ. Responsible action has to be contextual
because "we do not ourselves create the conditions of our action."[19] We are limited by the responsibilities of the neighbor
who confronts us, acts towards us and responds to our actions
toward him.[20] We are limited by both God and neighbor who
confront us in Christ and constitute both the origin and the
limits of our action.[21] In this setting, the Christian is called to
be concerned both with intention and result. He is summoned
to weigh the circumstances and to do the possible, ignoring his
own goodness or evil. "The man who acts ideologically sees

himself justified in his idea; the responsible man commits his action into the hands of God and lives by God's grace and favour."[22]

Bonhoeffer recognizes that what he calls "pertinence" (the word he uses to describe the Christian's responsible relation to things) clashes with principle when the necessities of human life conflict with exact adherence to a formal law of state, commerce or family.[23] In the face of a necessity that "knows no law," the responsible agent finds his choices limited and may have to resort to irrational action such as war or breach of treaty in politics or destruction of livelihoods in economics. Bonhoeffer cautions, however, that the greatest evil which can result from recognition of these peripheral cases is to make a norm of the exceptional, for responsible action acknowledges the validity of law even in the breach of it.[24] If this stress on the specific person in his unique situation sounds individualistic and relativistic, Bonhoeffer's answer is that the church is the point of departure for Christian ethics and that the self acts within a certain context which is held in common by many.

Paul Lehmann's contextualism has a theological base which is virtually the same as Bonhoeffer's. He has more to say in his ethical writing about the *koinonia* context, but due to Bonhoeffer's great concern with the church in such writings as *Sanctorum Communio* and *Act and Being,* we cannot say that he ties ecclesiology and ethics together any more than the German martyr does. Lehmann accents the indicative, not the imperative. As with Bonhoeffer and H. Richard Niebuhr, God's will is seen more as the action than the demand of God. Christian ethics is descriptive rather than prescriptive. It is "oriented toward revelation and not toward morality."[25] The ought cannot be ignored by Lehmann's admission, but he comes close to doing so. For him, "What am I to do?"—not "What ought I to do?"—should be the Christian's leading question. Like Bonhoeffer, Lehmann presents a self who "plays it by ear" although he speaks not about hearing the command in the situation but about discerning and cooperating with what God is doing in the world "to make human life human."

In the *koinonia* a pattern of response is forged, but we are given little in the way of description of the pattern. Humanizing activity is highly exalted but scarcely defined. Maturity and "new humanity" have content for Lehmann, but it is hard to nail down. With Bonhoeffer, he is chary of moral principles because their use abstracts morality from life.[26] Lehmann places a great premium on the sensitivity which has a feel for the fitting in the situation. Rational reflection is conspicuous for its absence.

His accent is on freedom, but it is theonomous or obedient freedom. In response to the indicative of God's grace which has brought ethical claim and act together, freedom and obedience are united. Conscience, theonomously defined, knows the good in relation to God's action of humanization, rather than in relation to one's own morality, and does not surrender its freedom to the security of an absolute authority.[27] Truth telling decisions then for Lehmann as for Bonhoeffer are free as far as the facts are concerned, as in the case of the dying patient or used-car salesman in Lehmann's writing,[28] or the girl in school who is asked if her father is a drunkard in Bonhoeffer's, but they are subject to the reality revealed in Christ who is the truth. They are to be true to that reality and to a relationship, but not necessarily to the facts.

Helmut Thielicke's writing on borderline situations treats "improvisation in the moment."[29] Over against casuistic advance decisions, he emphasizes the simplification that will take place on the spot because "the antithesis between the kingdom of God and the power of the AntiChrist is plainly disclosed."[30] The free man in Christ can rely on the Spirit's presence to confer "the power of improvisation."[31] Unlike Lehmann, however, Thielicke emphasizes careful reflection in advance. He writes:

> This freedom is not . . . a blanket license to do whatever we want. It is not libertinism. Similarly, improvisation does not imply a mere vegetating indifference in respect of the moment. The best extemporaneous speakers are those who have prepared best and who, out of the clarity

which they have reached in meditation, give themselves to the moment and leave their notes behind. Hence Christian improvisation does not stand in antithesis to careful reflection. It is rather that freedom for the urgent claim of the moment which has been won by way of such reflection. It has nothing to do with a laissez faire approach or attitude.[32]

The improvisation of the moment may be mistaken; but under the freedom of the gospel which knows "that my salvation is no longer linked with conditional clauses,"[33] the self acts boldly in expectation of God's taking over his own cause and making the course clear. This confidence about clear guidance is similar to Bonhoeffer's.

H. Richard Niebuhr's radical monotheism and relational value theory underlie his brand of contextualism, but his social analysis of the self as answerer is also fundamental. Man is more basically a responder to actions on him in the context of his communities than he is an obeyer of rules or a pursuer of ends. Both rules and ends are abstract and once removed from the dialogue and demands of relationships. Niebuhr belongs with Bonhoeffer and Lehmann[34] in departure from the problem-solving model of ethical decision which is characterized by both Thomistic and Kantian applications of principles or laws to cases or problems. But he and Gustafson and others of his students really don't belong in the same bin with Bonhoeffer and Lehmann or with latter-day situationists like Robinson and Fletcher.

As Eleanor Haney has pointed out, in contrast to the problem-solving scheme of a natural-law thinker or a Protestant emphasizer of principles such as Edward Leroy Long, and to situationists' commitment of the self to the other in the moment as seen in Bonhoeffer, Lehmann, and Fletcher, such ethicists as H. Richard Niebuhr, James Gustafson, and Gordon Kaufman adopt what Dr. Haney calls a political approach. Here the stress is on interpretation of response to prior action on the self in a field of continuing interaction. Niebuhr has as many reservations as anyone about the abstraction of the Kantian or Thomistic approaches to ethics. He sees the responsible self entering into conversation which is already in progress and never "starts from scratch." Whereas the second group tends to isolate the moment and emphasize the discontinuity between situations, Niebuhr's existentialism underlines the importance both of what has happened and of what will or is expected to happen and also of the context of social solidarity which gives stability and continuity to context.

Bonhoeffer and Lehmann counteract the extremity of an existentialist ethic of a Sartrean variety through their stress on the church. Fletcher, although he eschews the Sartrean position as antinomian, has failed to reckon with the political or social nature of the self. On the one hand he reflects his Thomistic background. He defines conscience as "reason making moral judgments" and emphasizes applying love rationally in the situation. He speaks of justice often simply as "love using its head."[35] His social ethic is admittedly utilitarian and thus entails a kind of rational calculus. On the other hand his stress on the uniqueness of the situation fits him into the second category. In neither respect has he given evidence of an understanding of moral responsibility which escapes individualism and mere calculation. Fletcher offers us the alternatives of legalism, antinomianism, or his brand of situationism. These choices do not exhaust the options. H. Richard Niebuhr provides one clear alternative to Fletcher which falls into neither of the polar pitfalls which Fletcher abhors.

Fletcher and his somewhat less radical partner in popularization of "the new morality," Robinson, agree with the ethicists we have mentioned in rejection of any legalism which makes moral decisions in advance. Both reject listing of acts which are wrong in themselves without exception. Love is what makes an act right. Rightness, or wrongness, happens to an act; it is not resident in it. Although maxims (Fletcher) containing accumulated moral wisdom afford guidance, and a legal "net" (Robinson) provides a framework of conduct which is essential to social life, the maxims or laws must not be absolutized in such a way as to preclude the possibility of acting in the extreme situation in a fashion which is "against the rules." Fletcher seems to major in the exceptional to the neglect of the usual;

Robinson is more conservative with regard to traditional norms at the same time that he emphasizes the need to allow for extraordinary possibilities. For both men, Christian ethics is not a code of conduct but a mode of approaching decisions. The content varies with the situation; the conscience impelled by love alone is constant.

The rejection of a legal absolutism that straitjackets the moral life, which is shared by all the witnesses we have called, is sound enough. The rule-ruled life is hardly the Christian liberty of which Paul writes, and it would not be misrepresenting Jesus to have him say "The rules were made for man, not man for the rules." Rules can never capture the scope of the Christian's responsibility nor the creative possibilities of love. To revert to Bonhoeffer's illustration, abstinence from committing adultery does not begin to describe the morality of a marriage. The rule-reigned life leads either to the self-righteousness which thinks the rules have been kept or the despair of the scrupulously strict who knows they cannot be. Man in his sinful pride lets principles eclipse persons because making a name is more important than meeting his neighbor. We aim at being good, not recognizing that good is always relational. We mistake guiltlessness for goodness. The line from Shaw's play is apt. It is often hard to make progress when you're toeing a line. Ironclad rules do not allow for the exceptional. The crowning blow for the law is the lure of the forbidden. The Genesis depiction of the lure of the forbidden fruit is recalled in the objection of one lady to the Ten Commandments "because they put ideas in your head." Sin finds occasion in the law (Romans 7); the forbidden bids with greater strength.

Still another problem with principles or rules is that in a given decision, two or more values or standards may be in conflict and one must decide which one to weight the heaviest under the circumstances. In abortion cases the desire to preserve embryonic life must be weighed against the mother's physical and emotional health or perhaps against the likelihood of the "life" being a thalidomide baby. Some decisions to resort to violence are based on an exaltation of the rectification of injustice over the desire to preserve life. Resistance to tyrants may be at points given the Jeffersonian accolade as "obedience to God," although the resistance fighter may hate the bloodshed. Freedom and order are not always compatible in a given instance.

Achievement of partial results may dictate demanding less than what the politician considers ideal. Charles Weltner of Georgia courageously decided he could not compromise with hate and withdrew from the congressional race rather than give endorsement to a ticket headed by racist Lester Maddox. Another equally sensitive person might have decided to agree to the endorsement, "sit on his hands" during the race, and live to fight another day for causes for which congressmen from his state have infrequently crusaded. Men "of principle" often sneer at compromisers, but principles at times can be escape routes from responsibility. One must at times decide whether to witness to a value at the price of relevance or to accomplish something by not insisting on everything. The first can lead to a naive idealism which never touches the earth of political reality. The second leads to a cynical realism which never emerges from the dust and mud to look at the stars.

"The new morality" does not receive blanket approval because of its agreement with its concerns, which have been expressed. The pages of the proponents such as Lehmann, Fletcher, or Robinson are sadly lacking in definition either of love or of the situation. Of Fletcher, Gustafson observes that he does not designate what constitutes a "situation" and that his most radical statements are with regard to narrowly interpersonal or one-to-one neighbor relations. The time and space span is also restricted:

> If the situation is to determine what love requires, it is terribly important how one understands his situation. Is it boy plus girl between 1 A.M. and 3 A.M. after a number of drinks in a motel room who feel affection for each other stimulated by proper knowledge of erogenous zones? Or is it boy, responsible to others than the girl, and responsible to and for her over a long period of time under a covenant of some sort, plus girl concerned not only for the present moment but for the past and future rela-

tionships as well, in a human community for whose vitality and order they have responsibility and which in turn has to seek its common good?[36]

Love goes begging for pegging too. To quote Gustafson again, it is "a word that runs through Fletcher's book like a greased pig." He continues, "Nowhere does Fletcher indicate in a systematic way his various uses of it. It refers to everything he wants it to refer to." One unidentified quipster calls this "sloppy *agapé*." Lehmann's reticence about shading in the shape of "maturity" or "humanity" is more than matched by the vagueness of this thing called "love" in Fletcher and Robinson.

The way in which human prejudice can be read into the meaning of love is illustrated in a frightening way by the ardent anti-communist who exhorted a certain civic club to fight communism on the local level "using the Christian virtue love." According to him, this meant we must set to work to *L*ocate them, *O*bserve them, *V*erify our information, and then *E*radicate them. He hinted that we could look for them in religious groups and labor organizations who opposed his political-economic views of the national association which was sponsoring his public-relations tour. Such a view is far from those of Fletcher and Robinson, but it indicates the need for definition.

A further defect in "situational ethics" which has received fleeting mention already is its exaggeration of the novelty of each new decision-making situation. Continuities between moral moments and patterns of customary response are soft-pedaled, and the unprepared self is left to be utterly spontaneous in doing the loving thing which the context suggests. Lester Kirkendall argues effectively against the folly of seeing each decision-making situation as presenting "a wholly new set of circumstances." Many persons who attempt to operate this way "find themselves immobilized by the need to analyze each human relations situation from scratch." He continues,

> They are unsure in their decision-making as to what factors need to be taken into account. They are not clear as to the nature of love, or what it requires of them. So while they are tired of a legalistic interpretation of regulations

imposed by fiat, they are lost when it comes to knowing
how to proceed within the broad, ill-defined framework
of the situation ethicist.[37]

Kirkendall here has incisively connected the severance of situation with a fuzzy understanding of the meaning of love.

Calvin's three uses of the law are all neglected by "the new
morality." The Reformer affirmed the functions of the law as
convicter of sin, as orderer of society, and as guide to the
Christian life.[38] The new morality neglects all three functions
of law because it is so afraid that law has to be legalistic. The
third use as guide is asserted but soft-pedaled although some
other word for law or rule (such as "maxim") is preferred.
Appreciation for the extent to which the conscientious person
must often reflect on decisions in light of moral generalizations
or principles is, however, less lacking in Fletcher, who speaks
of prudent calculation of means for the ends of love, than in
Paul Lehmann, whose high premium on the spontaneous and
the almost-intuitive shortchanges rational deliberation in decision-making.[39]

The second use of law is asserted as a necessary "net," but
positive possibilities of the net are not accentuated. Concern
for order is viewed legalistically. The first use is sorely lacking.
One should love and do what he thinks best and not feel
guilty if a few rules are ruled out or the decision is ambiguous
at best. Fletcher asks, "Can we divorce right from good? Is
it true, as men sometimes say, that there are tragic situations
in which the best we can do is evil? Is it possible to say that
the *best* we can do (that is, the most loving thing possible for
the most neighbors) is wrong?"[40] It is interesting that Fletcher
should be concerned with assuring the act's "rightness" when
he is so approving of Bonhoeffer, who urges that we act as we
believe God is leading us and leave the judgment of rightness
to him. There is a difference between trying to be responsible
and trying to be "right." It needs also to be asked whether
an act which is "lovingly" done is beyond question. Certainly
the Christian should live on the forgiveness of one's sins, not
allowing yesterday's failures to cripple today's possibilities, and
surely the cautious subservience to little legalisms has restricted

rather than inspired responsibility for the neighbor in many cases. However, there is still a place for remorse and bad conscience in discipleship. We can too easily assume that our love is unalloyed and that we acted upon it without having any second thoughts about our self-deception and blundering. Of Fletcher, Gustafson observes, "He seems to want an ethic that omits any possibility of a bad conscience. He has unwarranted confidence in the directing and informing power of love . . . He does not want people wallowing in guilty feelings for having made moral mistakes."[41]

Wallowing does indicate an inverted pride which is as deadly as self-righteousness. One can exult in being "unholier than thou," too. The trouble with Fletcher is that he gives conscience too much rope for rationalization and negligible counsel to contrition. As Niebuhr points out, good conscience, understood as faith, and guilty conscience can coexist. Fletcher leaves the impression at points that the self can assume the rightness of its action if it acts in love. Bonhoeffer, whom Fletcher enjoys quoting on other points, opposes attempts to assess one's rightness, but he does not advocate a disregard of guilt—which he says can devastate the self.[42] Guilt feelings are not all foolishness, and one seeks to ignore them at risk of disaster. It is cynicism, according to Bonhoeffer, to fail to recognize one's guilt in the breach of law.[43] Actions in accordance with the law as ultimate authority as well as actions in free responsibility which may at times break the law are guilty, and the agent can live only by God's forgiveness. Disintegration—loss of integrity—results. The hope is that integrity will be conceived less and less in terms of self-centered conscientiousness and more and more in terms of that responsibility for the neighbor which will accept the burden of guilt and freedom when necessary.

Obedience and the Obligational

Changing our direction, we turn now to an assessment of contributions on the other side (but not necessarily by different people) which may serve as correctives for the distortions

of some brands of situationalism. Here the approaches are as
varied as are emphases on the situational. John Bennett advocates "middle axioms" for making love more definite; Paul
Ramsey seeks principles which best embody love in relation to
a given problem (such as the principles of non-combatant im-
munity and proportionality *vis à vis* warfare). James Gustafson
is working with fidelity and obligation in personal relations as
components of love. He supposes that the "new moralists" like
so many before them think that obligation implies law and is
thus antithetical to an ethics of grace,[44] of grateful response to
the action of God. Those who either believe or imply that the
Christian life is all freedom and spontaneity often neglect the
dutiful and obligatory side of the covenanted relationship with
God and neighbor. Gustafson warns,

> In the time of a "new morality" that comes into being
> under Christian auspices, a morality that smacks of a kind
> of shallow concern with self-realization, it is perhaps
> even more important to see the significance of the struc-
> ture of personal relations as a structure of mutual obliga-
> tions of persons to each other and for the consequences of
> their common life.[45]

When concern about consequences often goes no further
than the hope that no one gets hurt and when structures of
relation are either viewed as temporary or as overly binding,
the aspects of responsibility, fidelity, and obligation in interpersonal relations are in need of reaffirmation. It is disturbing
that there are circles in which one can be hissed for using the
word *responsibility* because it is so laden with pejorative connotations.

Marriage is but one example of Gustafson's reminder that
"responsibility for each other is a structure of love, not merely
the occasion for love."[46] Marriage also illustrates the way in
which obligation—a stronger word than responsibility according to Gustafson—enters into life in community. A covenant
bond makes claims of steadfastness on the parties to it. "To
be for the other person is to delight in his presence; it is also
to be responsible for him, to be obligated to him."[47]

These structures of obligation are not necessarily a kind of hurdle in spite of which two or more people love each other. They are potentially the occasions for the expression of love, the context in which love can flower. Because relationships are complex and because societies feel the need of formalizing structures for the well-being of all, laws and traditions develop as ground rules and guides. These can be rigorous and unduly restrictive, or they can be salutary restraints. Structures are not to be accepted uncritically. We have a right to ask "Why?" But often there are good reasons why. People who know the meaning of living in covenant will know that, but their numbers are all too few.

One of the aspects of fidelity on which we depend in our society is the mutual trust that we can believe each other when we talk and act. To a large extent our financial transactions presume on the dependability of the neighbor's word or check. The distress over the credibility gap is the uneasiness of wondering whether our elected officials are leveling with us. Imagine a society—and there are such in the world—where the credibility gap was a gulf not just in government but everywhere, where one presumed in all his relationships that "being taken in" was the rule and honesty was the exception, where there was no assurance of mail delivery. Consider the society where totalitarian ideology propounds the big lie until the truth is no longer recognizable. Picture relations where no one's "word is his bond." One can recognize the possibility of the need for the loving lie, but he should also recognize that the very possibility of its effectiveness rests on credibility. The German fishing-boat master[48] during World War II who was helping smuggle Jews out of Germany could not have convinced the port inspector that he had no escapees below decks if the port inspector had not trusted him.

One of Bonhoeffer's insights is apt here. He speaks of hallowing the law even in breaking it.[49] One is free from keeping the Sabbath or honoring parents (see Jesus' breaches of these commandments) or from the whole divine law if one acts for the sake of God and neighbor—thereby for the sake of Christ.

This freedom, however, only confirms or serves the true fulfillment of the law in breaking it. One may at times lie but for
the sake of a higher truth. He may kill—to preserve life. He
may steal—still affirming that the neighbor's property is to be
respected.[50]

Society does rely on tacit trust in many ways, but it also
knows that legal sanctions are necessary not only for the provision of common understanding about social structure but also
as a dike against sin. In case people practice hoodwinking in
ways that are socially devastating, restraints are present with
more force than a frown. Truth-in-packaging and truth-in-lend-
ing bills are current expressions of need for sterner sanctions
on irresponsibility. Laws and other social structures and restraints stand as warnings to the self concerning the boundaries
of toleration for dereliction in obligation. To paraphrase Reinhold Niebuhr, man's capacity for fidelity or truthfulness makes
community possible; his inclination to rationalize his interests
makes community constraint necessary. In this light the "must"
demands of conscience may be immature psychologically, but
they may also be salutary socially in the absence of sufficient
inner "oughts."

This need for restraint against rationalization is often ignored by "the new morality" in its preoccupation with attacking legalism—an onslaught which at times appears to be "beat-
ing a dead horse." The situationists are long on the redeeming
work of God which liberates and inspires; they are short on the
ordering and governing work of God which enables and sustains
community life and judges man's sinful self-assertion. When we
consider the list of evils perpetrated with sincere conviction,
we can appreciate checks on our erroneous judgments and inclinations. H. Richard Niebuhr and James Gustafson aid us
by underscoring the positive possibilities for God's work through
institutions and customs and laws as well as the need occasioned
by man's sin. Emil Brunner and Helmut Thielicke by contrast
fall into the dualistic wrath-love split, to which Luther tended
and which makes God's governing only negative and sin-cen-
tered and makes institutions the handiwork only of God's "left
hand."

Bonhoeffer's counter for a freedom which makes love too shapeless is obedience, which he couples with freedom in responsibility. In the eloquent statement which stands at the beginning of this chapter, Bonhoeffer describes the responsibility which is both obedient and free and cautions against the pitfalls of reductionisms on either side. He presents obligation more in terms of law than of fidelity and there is something of the same uneasy truce between obligation or obedience and freedom as there is between conscience and responsibility in Christ. Yet he is getting at the same irresponsible freedom which Gustafson criticizes, and both of these men are from the camp of the contextualists. To quote Bonhoeffer:

> Responsibility and freedom are corresponding concepts. Factually, though not chronologically, responsibility presupposes freedom and freedom can consist only in responsibility. Responsibility is the freedom of men which is given only in the obligation to God and to our neighbour.
>
> The responsible man acts in the freedom of his own self, without the support of men, circumstances or principles, but with a due consideration for the given human and general conditions and for the relevant questions of principle.[51]

Bonhoeffer emphasizes that no law binds the Christian agent, only his obligation to God and neighbor which is perfect freedom. Without claiming absolute knowledge of good and evil or attempting self-justification, he can choose among rights and among wrongs where the relativities and limitations of a situation call for such action. He trusts that God's guidance is a factor in the action and that ultimately his responsible obedience is in a real sense God's deed. Tension there may well be between obedience and freedom as between conscience and responsibility, but responsibility holds together both law and liberty. To allow either to slip away would lead either to irresponsible, individualistic license or to dreary, dutiful dependence. Whether one acts under obligation or in freedom, he leaves himself and his action in God's hands.

Bernhard Häring appreciates the contributions of Christian existentialism and personalism as correctives to legalism, but

he attacks situationism. To him, the situational reaction is a
needed criticism of a rationalistic "ethic of essences," but he
cautions that a "substratum of essence" must be maintained.
Love is not, as Fletcher would have it, "the only absolute."[52]
One does not have to choose between situation and standard.
The strengths of both positions can be joined, as Häring sees
it. Theistic morality can stress both individuality and the continuity of a person with his acts.

God's eternal law or design for all actions and movements
can be known by reason (natural law), but sin makes divine
law revealed in scripture necessary for clarification. The minimal standards for human behavior furnished by this law safe-
guard the freedom of the children of God and are not to be
disobeyed. There are intrinsically and unconditionally evil actions such as lying, adultery, and unjust attack (all of which
take some defining, especially the last one) which violate the
absolute values of truth, fidelity, and justice. These universals,
however, only set boundaries and cannot comprehend the infinite variety of selves and situations. There is large leeway
within which conscience must decide on the implications of
the norms in the situation. Häring urges that since the natural
law is unformulated, it must be read anew in each situation.[53]
This reading requires what Häring calls a "tactful conscience":

> Knowledge of the universal law must preserve (the self)
> from seeing his own self-interest in the law. But vital
> morality demands more than mere acquaintance with the
> norms of law, it demands the fine delicacy of tactful con-
> science, the sense of the particular and special, which goes
> beyond mere knowledge of the law. This is prudence.[54]

Though not *under* law, the Christian obeys the law from
within in love, which has been poured into his heart through
the Holy Spirit. He goes beyond the law in love, but he does
not violate the law. Häring criticizes Protestantism for seeing
law mainly as accuser, a charge which is more aptly made
against Luther than against Calvin (although Häring does not
say so).[55] Against this negative assessment, he asserts that law's
primary purpose is "to direct us to right understanding of the

divine will in its loving summons."⁵⁶ The doctrine, precepts, and example of the whole church and the divine revelation to Israel and in Christ afford the Christian infallible guidance with respect to ultimate matters and basic principles. On less than ultimate matters and in the application of basic norms, the self must exercise prudence; and conflict may legitimately arise between the conscientious judgment of the individual and non-infallible ecclesiastical rulings. Morality based on principles as in the church's casuistry prepares the way for the judgment of prudence in the situation.⁵⁷

A cultivated prudence, together with the gifts of the Holy Spirit which perfect that wisdom, tunes the self both to the loving voice of God and the call of "the hour." Prudence implements the law of love in the situation. Without love, prudence is only shrewdness. Without prudence, love is inept and naive. Conscience (as *synteresis*) urges the demand that the good be done, and prudence discerns how the command is to be obeyed concretely. Conscience furnishes the compulsion; prudence supplies the content. Conscience makes prudential judgment imperative.⁵⁸ The acts of prudence are the acts of *conscientia,* the other aspect of conscience in Thomistic thought. Where conscience is prudent, the two are the same. If the voice of conscience is not the voice of prudence, it is not the voice of God. However, if the heart is in the right place and the virtue of prudence is well developed, *synteresis* and *conscientia* are united in disposition toward and implementation of the love of God. This is the combination Jesus extolled—the wisdom of the serpent and the innocence of the dove.

Häring's praise of prudence is valuable filler for what is often a gap in Protestant ethical theory as well as for a tendency toward heedless spontaneity in some "new moralists." The attempts of the politically naive to relate the gospel to the facts of social life have often traveled on those infamous paving stones—good intentions, and the results have frequently been the reverse of what was proposed. The experience of getting one's hands burned in such conscientious crusades has occasioned many a transition from sentimental attempts to save the world to cynical or pious abdication from involvement and responsibility.

Häring's effort to combine situation and standard demonstrates a certain independence from some of the rigid rejections of situational concerns in his tradition. His positive assessment of law is refreshing in contrast to the negativism of the situationists and in light of the Psalmist's joy in it.[59] However, there is a static abstractness about his absolute values, a recurrent concern for risk reduction and being right, and an authoritarian view of church authority in his thought which pushes further toward restrictive legalism than we can go. Häring has shown growing openness and flexibility, but his treatment of moral selfhood in *The Law of Christ* still presents a straitjacket of absolute rules though with a significantly looser fit.

Reversion to an issue of truth telling illustrates his restriction of the scope of freedom and his static and abstract view of values (as opposed to the dynamism and concreteness of relational thinking). Whereas Bonhoeffer makes truth telling a matter of being true to a relationship in a situation,[60] and Lehmann, with Bonhoeffer, speaks of saying "the right word" or "the living word" in the context,[61] Häring deems telling a lie an essential violation of the value of truth.[62] For Bonhoeffer and Lehmann, truth is concretely interpreted; for Häring it is an abstract, and it would seem, absolute value.

Covenantal Context and Content

From this assessment of situationism, it can be concluded that the bounds of the situation often need pushing out and the bones of words such as *love, maturity, new humanity* and *will of God* need some filling out—not in rigid exhaustive fashion, but in descriptive and illuminative ways. Covenant is basically relational, but covenant obligation has content. Content and context need not be antithetical. Content can be conceived dynamically rather than statically. Principles can be illuminative rather than prescriptive. Law, as Thielicke puts it, can be normative without being regulative.[63] One need not choose between being an absolute legalist and an utter relativist. A pluralist, which is Gustafson's designation of himself, brings a number of principles with him to his decisions, no one of which is declared in advance to be inviolable.

Christian conscience can respond to the living God in light of both tradition and situation. When context is conceived broadly enough, it will include content, generalizations, patterns, and characteristics of a Christian style of life. When rules are set in the context of the action of a living God and of unique persons and situations, their limitations become apparent and the importance of sensitivity, creativity, and responsible spontaneity in the Christian life comes to the fore. Christian conscience expresses both consensus and individuation.[64] Members of communities have a common history, but each person also has a unique history and interacts with his social milieu in a unique way.

Conscience, as here understood, has to do with one's orientation, one's ultimate commitments, one's habitual style of life from within which specific consciously weighed decisions are made. The quality of one's relationships and the nature of one's dispositions are of a piece with individual decisions. One's ultimate commitments are choices, and one's choices reflect where one's commitments lie as a moral agent. Conscious choices may reflect unconsciously espoused values or rules. To stress intuition and sensitivity in the specific decisions one consciously makes is not to cut the acting self off from the nexus of its personal history which brings patterns of action and appropriated principles to decisions. In like manner, emphasis on love's sensitivity in the situation, however well backed up with guidance from communal context, must not be allowed to submerge the significance of this rational weighing of alternatives and the use of law by the Christian in his decision making, both as a dike against sin and as a guide. The context of *koinonia* gives a feel for the appropriate. It shapes a self which reacts instinctively to certain obligations, but it also furnishes tools for rational discussion and deduction. Prudence in the situa-

tion involves sensitivity, but also requires sagacity. Its wisdom
instructs love. Its love inspires and directs its discernment.

Prudence, properly understood, can serve as a corrective
to any notion that a choice must be made by the Christian
moral agent between reason and response in the situation, between reflection and spontaneity. Häring and Josef Pieper have
both given a situational slant to prudence. Just as Jacques
Maritain and Pope John XXIII represent a swing in contemporary Catholicism toward existentially determined moral regula-
tions hammered out in the midst of the moral struggle and
away from abstract principles deduced casuistically from natural law, so prudence is being depicted as an ability to read
the situation insightfully, as worldly-wisdom, not as abstract
programmatic knowledge to be put into procrustean practice.[65]
Response in the situation cannot be abstractly calculated in
advance, but neither should it be heedlessly unreflective as
Bonhoeffer seems to indicate. Lehmann too is short on the
demands of disciplined reflection. The necessity of discerning
how God is at work "making human life human" implies the need
for sagacity as well as sensitivity. To accomplish a union of
tough-mindedness and tender-heartedness the hymn might better urge us to "*wise* up, O men of God" if we are to "give
heart and soul and *mind* and strength to serve the King of
kings." Such sanctified shrewdness steers between the naively
inept good intentions of the loving but ignorant and the cynic-
ally realistic resourcefulness of the wily but worldly. It also
steers between permissiveness and prescription.

Sallie TeSelle presents the Christian's dilemma on this score
in these words:

> It is the problem of making love realistic and appropriate
> but not undercutting its spontaneity, of instructing the
> total inclination of the self toward God and toward other
> men but not crystallizing that inclination into a program
> of action. It is the problem of informed love.

Mrs. TeSelle continues by indicating that the three most important forms of instruction in the New Testament (the "confession," as seen in Paul's letters, the "parable," as seen in the

teachings of Jesus, and "the story of Jesus," as seen in the Synoptics' portrait of Jesus) are in the same mode, "one that informs by concrete acquaintance with reality, the reality of man with God and of man with man,"[66] one that informs through "felt" knowledge, not through rules or programs.

Just as appreciation of the guidance afforded by ethical generalizations does not justify absolutizing them, so recognition of the individuation of conscience should not justify privatizing it. As stated earlier, one of the ways of wisdom is verification of one's conscientious verdict by checking it against the conscientious commitments, concerns, and decisions of other Christians, living and dead. It is at this point that a conditional, not an absolute casuistry may be helpful. Protestant ethical theory has often eschewed all casuistry for fear of absolutizing it, but in practice Protestants have relied on the guidance of other Christians with regard to certain types of situations and common social problems.

The church does provide an objective reference for moral decisions which escapes both the subjectivity of autonomous individualism and the domination of heteronomous collectivism, which is neither anomic relativism or rigid absolutism. As the whole argument of Bonhoeffer's *Act and Being* insists, in the church we can affirm the givenness of God's revelation without denying God's freedom, we can affirm both continuity and discontinuity, both immanence and transcendence, both being and act, both "the 'constancy and continuity of the divine command,' which demands a continuity in man's response" and existential decisions of the moment.[67]

In Rolf Hochhuth's play *The Deputy*, Gerstein, the Protestant who is working against Hitler within the SS, gives an intriguing answer to Riccardo, the priest who is likewise zealous for the defeat of Hitler:

> Riccardo: It's difficult, yes, Herr Gerstein.
> What does your conscience say?
> Gerstein: Conscience? Who could trust that!
> Conscience or God:
> men never have wreaked such havoc

> as when invoking God—or an idea.
> Conscience is a treacherous guide. I am
> convinced that Hitler acts according to his
> conscience. No, I need an answer from outside
> myself. We Protestants depend too much
> upon ourselves. One cannot always bear it.
> Don't we, indeed, have every ground to
> doubt . . . ? But answer me with the objectivity
> only a priest can have: what must I do?[68]

Here is the expressed need for objective reference to hold one on course against the winds of subjectivism, but Gerstein asked for help that was in fact not an answer. He requested a priestly prescription which would make the decision for him. The guidance he sought would have taken the burden of choice from him. Communal conscience stands between the errors both of the individualism which Gerstein feared in Protestantism and the authoritarianism which looked inviting to him in Roman Catholicism.

The disconcerting thing about seeking counsel from fellow Christians is that Christians equally convinced in conscience stand on different sides of many issues, usually convinced that their stand is supported by the testimony of scripture or the majority of Christians or the "best" Christians. Yet the plentiful evidence that conscience is not an infallible guide can hardly justify the scuttling of conscience as guide. Rather the Christian can allow for the honest differences of others, be mindful both of his sinfulness and theirs, and constantly check his views against those whose consecrated wisdom has been found sound on other occasions. In this connection, Bonhoeffer suggestively advocated a certain suspicion of one's habitual stance. The conservative must beware of his habitual refusal to oppose the status quo, while the revolutionary must beware of automatically making a radical response on every question.[69] The self's zealous or cautious impulses are not to be neatly equated with the call of Christ.

Reinhold Niebuhr's test of tolerance commends itself as a precaution against such equations and also as a corrective to the inaction which revels in relativism. In *The Nature and*

Destiny of Man he posits that tolerance should include both (1) the humble awareness of one's fallibility which checks the notion that one has all the answers and (2) an unmitigated zeal with regard to the commitments one conscientiously makes with the light he has.[70] Such tolerance precludes the uncompromising cocksureness of the fanatical conscience or what T. V. Smith calls "a little totalitarian operating in the bosom of every conscientious man, especially if he is a middle man operating in the name of God."[71] It also avoids the paralysis of the perplexed conscience which is so overwhelmed by the relativities of the self's knowledge of truth and right that action is endlessly deferred.

The Christian conscience does have content which is continuous within the Christian community, both past and present. Spelling out that content in any but the most general terms gets to be perilous in a hurry. What can be said of this content? For one thing, there is continuity between this content or consensus and the ethical generalizations of other communities. As James Gustafson recently wrote,

> The criteria of Christian conduct are not necessarily exclusive of the criteria defined by other communities or other moralists. Many particular considerations are shared between Western humanists and Christians, between political philosophers and theologians. But not every assertion of every moralist can be absorbed into the criterion of Jesus Christ.[72]

Gustafson cautions that "not every assertion of every moralist can be absorbed into the criterion of Jesus Christ" and mentions racist morality, whether of Nazi or White Citizens Council variety, as "clearly antagonistic to the principal considerations given in the Christian gospel." He is affirming that there are generalizations which human experience has found to be the *sine qua non* of corporate life. These enjoy an impressive consensus, if not a universal acknowledgment. Bonhoeffer and Richard Niebuhr both refer to this continuity between communities and between sinner and saint. Bonhoeffer speaks of "fundamental features of the law of life."[73] Niebuhr feels that natural law only becomes meaningful in terms of the lessons of social experience rather than in terms of static content which the rational can apprehend.

With Lehmann, Ebeling does not espouse a natural law doctrine. He is more concerned to stress the individuation of the conscience, with the content being supplied by situation and training, than the continuity among consciences from diverse communities. However, the four compulsions Ebeling finds in man, who is above all co-human, might supply a base from some consensus on the requirements of corporate life, and he mentions the maintenance of the humanity of human life through a legal minimum. Häring, of course, speaks from a natural-law tradition. He destroys the caricature of natural law as a code written on the mind, but his orientation is less social than teleological. The foundation of natural law is the tendency in man toward the good and his intuitive awareness that good should be sought and evil avoided. Certain tendencies belong to human nature as such. Without denying a tendency in man toward what he conceives to be the good for him, which may not be good at all, we are with Niebuhr in stressing social mediation more than teleological direction, the functional prerequisites of society more than the natural knowledge of rationality. This is not to say that the two emphases are mutually exclusive. Daniel Callahan in his article "Cosmic Purpose and Self-Identity" argues persuasively that man needs grounding in some cosmic purpose, some transcendent meaning, as well as identification within a human community in order to find himself fully.[74]

In the attempt to do justice to the Roman Catholic position and to illustrate further the social approach to natural law here suggested, we cite the outstanding Roman Catholic theologian Michael Novak. Following John Cogley, John Courtney Murray, Don Oden Lottin, and Bernard Lonergan, Novak wants it made clear "that natural law is not immutable and 'out there' but is developing and intrinsic to man's active and inventive intelligence."[75] He continues, "There are unchanging *principles* of natural law only in the sense in which *operations of intelligence* are principles, not in the sense in which *proposi-*

tions, precepts or premises are principles."[76] For this view, natural law roots in man's desire (1) for self-preservation, (2) for intellectual inquiry, (3) for social creativity and conversation, and (4) for God. Out of these roots could grow a plant with strong resemblance to ours, depending on where the emphasis is placed. However, when Novak spells out the operations of this law, the scientific model preempts the social. The rational overshadows the relational. The operations are: "experience that raises questions; inquiry that terminates in insight; further inquiry that tests insights against evidence; and decisions whether or not to act according to such experience, insight, and evidence."[77]

The position we are suggesting is not a denial of the validity or usefulness of Novak's but an affirmation of an emphasis we feel should be primary. According to traditional Thomistic doctrine on natural law, man is basically teleological rather than deontological. We are following Niebuhr and positing that man's tendencies and ends and his law and order are rooted in his basic or primordial sociality. The continuity between communities as to their ethical standards or systems is best approached in terms of the functional prerequisites of society rather than the functional operations of the intellect.

The question arises as to the relation between natural morality or the humanitarian consensus, which is found in operation in other communities than the Christian fellowship, and Christian revelation. Given the agreements between Christian and non-Christian, what does the Christian faith add or change about ethical systems which are obviously antithetical to common decency, as Nazism was? James Gustafson puts the crux of the matter in a sentence: "Christian morality is distinguished not by each particular detail but by the ultimate loyalty, and therefore the ultimate criterion, under which it brings all relative criteria."[78] This change in ultimate loyalty, which comes with faith in the Christian revelation, transforms natural morality, but not first of all, if at all, by providing new moral codes. However distorted by sin they are, laws enough are available to man.

The distinction between the Christian and the socially-concerned atheist, for instance, is often not discernable in their actions. They may conscientiously do exactly the same things (and individual Christians may "conscientiously" act in ways so different as to be irreconcilable with the actions of other conscientious Christians). What distinguishes the Christian and atheist who are partners in the struggle for racial justice or world peace or victory over poverty is the total context in which they act. Michael Novak has used the term *horizon* in the same way in which Lehmann speaks of the larger context of the action of God. Writes Novak,

> What distinguishes Christians is that their actions occur within the unlimited horizon of Christ's understanding and loving. Within that horizon their own present horizon is ever "under judgment." Their judge lives within them, calmly disclosing their insufficiencies. They must gradually "grow up into the stature of Christ."[79]

The Christian feels that the atheist's horizon is limited even though he may follow Christ as teacher. Christ is not for the believer merely a pattern but also a presence. In a sense, a Christian's action is Christ's action. The difference in the content of a Christian's action, as contrasted with the morality-sensitive atheist is often symbolic rather than propositional. To quote Novak again:

> Christians believe that Christ has spoken most adequately of the symbolic content of life in history.
>
> . . . .
>
> The difference [between Christian and atheist] is not in the external act or the historical effect but in its symbolic content. Believers and nonbelievers *do* the same things; they interpret their lives differently. Perhaps (as Daniel Callahan has noted) after two or three generations of widespread atheism, the difference between Christian and atheistic symbols will lead to increasingly divergent courses of action.[80]

He is saying that the non-Christian conscience may often be living on borrowed Christian capital. Novak further elaborates the different contexts of the two consciences:

... God—through events in our lives, Scriptures, life in
the church, conscious response to the sacraments—illumi-
nates our understanding of this world and enlarges our
capacity to love it, so that we, too, pierced by its beauty,
might be willing to die for it.

The atheist, through other events, books, communities,
is pierced by the earth's beauty and dies for it without
recognizing the significance Christians give it: that it is
man's, and we are Christ's and Christ is God's.[81]

Although revelation transforms rather than transmits moral
law, the moral law is made more imperative, more extensive
and more intensive by revelation, and man is given a new possibility of obedience in freedom. These themes are spelled out
in telling fashion by H. Richard Niebuhr in *The Meaning
of Revelation*.[82] He describes the way in which the imperative of
the moral law is made more imperative by God's indicative in
Christ thus:

Through the revelation of God the moral law is known
as the demand of one from whom there is no flight,
who respects no persons, and makes no exceptions, whose
seriousness of purpose will not suffer that his work be destroyed by the evasions and transgressions of this pitiful
and anarchic creature who sets up his little kingdom in
rebellion against God's sovereignty, and proclaims ever
new Messiahs to lead him to new disasters in the name of
his own righteousness. Transgressions of our law no
longer appear as acts which go against the grain of our nature, or of our social, or biological life; to be sure they do
all these things, but primarily they go against the grain of
the universe. Transgressions do not merely break the law
of conscience or of our society or even of life, but the law
of the beginner and perfector of all that is. They do not
merely violate the soul and body of the self or its community; they do violence to the body of God; it is his son who
is slain by our iniquity.[83]

Thus the core issue lies deeper than the superficialities of
disobedience and obedience to moral law. The basic problem
is one of idolatry rather than of conformity or non-conformity
to moral standards. For the sake of whom does one preserve
life, respect persons, keep promises, or give the cup of cold

water? Why does one not steal or commit adultery? What is the final referent of a person's morality? To whom is his final allegiance given in his observance of or deviation from or application of the traditional standards of his groups? If God is one's sovereign he is constrained to certain ways of relating to his neighbors, not primarily by mutual self-interest or common decency or enlightened judgment but in love of the Lord his God with his whole being.

Not only is the moral law made more imperative by God's revelation; it is also made more extensive and intensive.[84] All being is included, even enemies and sparrows and gardens. The inner man as well as his social behavior is covered. Revelation makes the moral law cut deeper in its condemnation of our irresponsibility and stretch farther in its obligation to responsibility. It deprives us all of our self-made limits of vocation, for instance. A physician is thus made responsible not only for his patients, but also for opposing conditions which threaten human life or medical science in his town, state, nation, or world. Bonhoeffer affirms, "Vocation is responsibility and responsibility is a total response of the whole man to the whole of reality; for this very reason there can be no petty and pedantic restricting of one's interests to one's professional duties in the narrowest sense."[85] There is such a thing as no overzealous extension of responsibility as well as legalistic restriction. The attempt to do everything is to make the world one's parish literally. The command of Christ directs specific responsibility, but the Christian should not draw lines which restrict concern and inhibit free obedience beyond the boundaries of one's "station in life."

Reality reveals who a man is and thus unveils the corruptions of both him and his laws. In the case of many expressions of non-Christian morality, this universalization of the scope of responsibility and intensification of the demands on the inner man as well as his outer behavior is a change in the content of one's ethic which is now seen as external, as parochial and limited. Still there are those whose love is as deep and as encompassing as that for which the Christian gospel calls, but who either do not have the same or any theological basis or else lack awareness of that basis.

The greatest change which comes about through God's revelation in Jesus Christ is as Niebuhr puts it, "the conversion of the imperative into an indicative and of the law whose content is love into a free love of God and man."[86] The self stands in different relation to the law. Although the new possibility is more a matter of potentiality than of actuality, it marks "the beginning of a new understanding of the law and the beginning of a new life."[87] For the Christian, only this new possibility occasioned by the reconciling, undeserved love of God, which fills the gap between claim and act, enables the acceptance of the greater responsibility which is placed upon him to let love permeate him intensively and issue from him extensively.

The facets of this love are limitless. Niebuhr's description which is quoted at the beginning of this chapter is classic but admittedly not exhaustive. All the "fruits of the Spirit," all the Christian virtues (as Häring underlines), are expressions of it. It has the distinction of being "both absolute and relative";[88] it is relevant and required in every situation, but its expressions are an infinite variety depending on the situation. If we make love mean everything, however, we run the risk of its meaning nothing. It is inseparable from and yet distinguishable from other Christian virtues such as faith, which brings a perspective or world view or center to life, and hope which relates eschatology to ethics.

Two of the ways which have been suggested here for spelling out love's ramifications have been (1) in terms of fidelity and obligation and (2) in terms of universality of responsibility. Translation of the Hebrew word *chesed* seems to demand the coupling of *steadfast* with love; and the emergent biblical understanding of the scope of this characterization of God is that it is universal. These emphases will bring to love both structure and scope, both convenantal content and boundless communal context for responsibility. In fact, universal responsibility describes both content and context.

To exalt universal responsibility can be misleading if the

impression is given that one is to think only in terms of greater quantity of beings to care about. Such responsibility should spell the end of all boundaries to love and of all divisions of people into "us" and "them" so that "the bad guys" can be hated or ignored "conscientiously." It also entails a different quality of care for those within partial communities of family, work, and nation as well as for those with whom one's contacts are limited or less. Sin makes men and groups of men myopic so that the domain of their responsibility is constricted, but it also makes them blind and insensitive to what love permits and requires in their own homes, neighborhoods, associations, towns, and countries. Universality of context is not an abstraction but a perspective on the particular and concrete.

Universal responsibility which encompasses the totality of being can be quite different from the utilitarian calculus which Joseph Fletcher proposes as the decision-maker's friend. It suggests limits which are involved in the affirmation of all being. It calls into question the making of people mere means to some high end. Some illustrations may help to indicate the relevance of this reservation.

When one wants information from a captured enemy, where if anywhere would mere calculus of the greatest good for the greatest number draw lines on issues such as torturing the person with the information or torturing his wife or children before his eyes? Thielicke discusses the borderline situation where one would be attempting "to force and break the conscience which is commanding him to keep silence."[89] The refined scientific methods now available and employed can induce "supradimensional pain" which, as Thielicke observes, "simply eliminates the ego altogether."[90] It is not a matter of threat and promise, of bribery or appeal to self-preservation. The truth drug, too, "chemically destroys the person in the central being." Unlike temptation and coercion, these methods bypass one's humanity. The person is reduced to a mere means to an end. Thielicke believes that at this point the Christian owes the world the public confession that he is not "capable of anything." Although Thielicke would hold that a Christian can hate war and yet on occasion fight "in good conscience," as does this writer, he is insisting that there are some contingencies which are beyond the pale of "conflict situations." He explains,

> ... if as Christians we think that torture is at least conceivable—perhaps under the exigencies of an extreme situation—we thereby reduce man to the worth of a convertible means, divest him of the *imago Dei,* and so deny the first commandment. This denial can never be a possible alternative. It can never be the way out of a conflict. ...
>
> If Christians, then, are found championing as a fundamental possibility, or perhaps themselves using, torture or forensic narcoanalysis, the faith of those who see this is necessarily jeopardized and exposed to extreme offense, because for them the communion of saints is thereby given the appearance of a devilish caricature. Eternal as well as temporal issues are thus at stake here. But the eternal destiny of those about us can never be weighed on the same scales as the temporal fate of, for example, companions, wives, and children, as if both were on the same level. In such a situation, then, there can be no genuine conflict.[91]

Thielicke has raised a question of limits which will not furnish the vicarious thrills of the sexier strain of situationists, but he is urging a responsibility to humanity and to those who will be offended which draws some lines that Fletcher's position does not explicitly draw.

The potential destructiveness of modern weaponry also calls for the setting in advance of some kinds of limits on the use of nuclear weapons and other contemporary types of wholesale annihilation. Although Reinhold Niebuhr is wary of setting limits in advance, he states that "even a nation can purchase life too dearly."[92] If the drawing of the line is no more than the determination not to use the ultimate weapons first, this is still a line. "To play it by ear" in the situation could lead to almost anything once mutual annihilation started unless some thought about limitations had been taken. Every eventuality cannot be foreseen and prior refusal ever to use weapons makes their possession no deterrent to the opposition, but such convictions as the insistence on counter-force rather than counter-population deployment of tactical weapons is a small initial step toward making the world safe from total destruction.

Still another issue with which Christian ethics must deal is the matter of "test-tube babies" and eugenic engineering. To what extent is manipulation of the bottled baby brain-size and genetic makeup a violation of his personhood—potential though it is—that is intolerable? Is there a point at which we erect "no trespassing" signs on holy ground which even the proposed improvement of mankind or of his behavior cannot justify? To refuse to tamper with the natural is finally to reject all medicine and technology and to abdicate our responsibility to subdue the earth. But the potentiality of human capability can be realized without resorting to total control of persons. There is still a distinction between partnership with God's ongoing creation and playing God, though the lines are not always easy to draw. Unlike the instances in which the conscientious person may even resort to the use of violence even to the point of taking life, we are looking here not at a situation which is considered intolerable by the decision-maker who is seeking the lesser evil but at how far we will go in certain kinds of research, genetic engineering, and behavior control.

Writing recently on ethical guidelines for biotechnology, Gabriel Fackre cautions against the immorality of some foreseeable possibilities for the control of life. One "still very blue sky" is prenatal programming of value choices. He calls this "an unethical practice of the first rank." "One generation does not have the wisdom or the virtue unilaterally to decide the fate of another; the living must not foreclose the unborns' options."[93] A more immediate and equally unthinkable possibility is preventive manipulation of one person by another. Although instant pacification (using sprays, gases, or drugs) might be justified in extreme circumstances, preventive manipulation through electrode implantation, surgery, or chemical control is out for Fackre. The possibilities of abuse of such power over another are just too great. Devices for biotechnical self-control are quite another matter and hold out great promise. It appears that responsibility may need to dictate restraints of a very definite kind at some points in the face of the possibilities of a "brave new world."

The principle of universal responsibility also affords the Christian a way of measuring his choices in those situations where the interests of many are involved and the interests of all cannot be given first priority. He cannot accept or express full responsibility for all of being all of the time, and certain priorities go along with one's place of responsibility. The criteria chosen for weighing the interests to be served should neither be self-serving in forgetfulness of others, nor other-serving in forgetfulness of the self one is called to be. (One can be sensitive to another's conscience without being bound by its judgments, as Paul suggested to the Corinthians with reference to meat offered to idols.) To the extent that his integrity is constituted in the God and Father of Jesus Christ rather than in those gods toward which to be conscientious is to be irresponsible, the Christian will be drawn where the need is greatest and where he finds coincidence of the larger number of legitimate interests.

There is another kind of coincidence, which promotes a union of norm and necessity and which is becoming increasingly real. This is the growing interdependence of peoples not just in a family or a town but in a nation and in the world. Fidelity cannot be forced perhaps, but society has always insisted legally and otherwise that minimal obligations be met. In an age when technology reduces distances daily, the facts of life in a shrinking and tangled world will foster broader considerations than people have sometimes had formerly. When a girl refuses to protest a fourth year of 11:15 lunch in her high school because she knows a change on the programming of the computer for setting a schedule would disrupt everybody's schedule, a new ethic is emerging. When television reveals man's inhumanity to man around the world, it makes some sheriffs more reticent to call out the dogs and some citizens have new thoughts about their nation's wars.

If the threat of publication is not sanction enough for sanity, our age knows too well the threat of annihilation. What Winston

Churchill called "the peace of mutual terror" describes a situation internationally in which the great powers have significantly modified their aims in the conflict between communism and Western-style democracy because of the horrible consequences nuclear weapons could bring. Coexistence and tolerance then can be the fruits of fear as well as the results of friendship.

There is a push toward a universality of responsibility which is built into our revolutionary age, and this cultural fact will have effects on the conscience of persons. However, progress toward universal concern and greater recognition of obligation within relationship is by no means inevitable. What we have been concerned about is this conversion and nurture of conscience by a power other than the force of circumstance. The choice between recognition of interdependence or "reaping the whirlwind" does not insure that men will exchange love for hate and indifference. Without the leaven of love, the nudge of necessity is a fragile hope. Some more durable and sound ground must be found for the construction of peace.

Conclusion

This study has been an effort to extend the lines of the contemporary Christian discussion of conscience and responsibility which has been greatly enriched by the thought of Bonhoeffer, Ebeling, Gustafson, Häring, Lehmann, H. Richard Niebuhr, and others. Building on the premise that human existence is primarily social, to use Niebuhr's designation, or linguistic, to use Ebeling's term, the implications of social selfhood for an understanding of conscience have been investigated, using the term *responsibility* as a way of relating conscience and community, or the self and its societies. Christian conscience has been distinguished in terms of the center of the self's integrity and loyalty, in terms of one's relation to the ultimate "Other" in the inner dialogue of the self, in terms of the community in which the primary social context for conscience is located, and in terms of the self-image or image of man one adopts. The Christian conscience then is a knowing with oneself or an integrity of heart in which the self's integrity or image of itself is constituted in God as he has made himself and true manhood known in Jesus Christ and as this revelation is mediated through the Christian community. The joint authorship of conscience, i.e., the self-in-the-Christian-community and the Christian-community-in-the-self, points to and is derived from a transcendent theonomous authority. Because the God to whom man is ultimately accountable is known in Christ as friend, his judgment is known to be gracious. In sin, by contrast, the self attempts to have its own independent conscience or makes some other center of value besides God its authority. Conscience as sinful is then legalistic, libertine, or idolatrous instead of covenantal or reconciled to God.

The conscience which is self-knowledge in relation to God or responsible integrity in God is conditioned and informed by the Christian community. This objective referent enables the avoidance of the polar pitfalls of collective, heteronomous absolutism and individual, autonomous antinomianism. This is so, on the one hand, because the church points beyond itself to its Sovereign, who alone is good and whose authority makes relational all human rule and rules. Only what love of God and neighbor requires is the absolute norm for the Christian. On the other hand, the context provided by the Christian community excludes autonomous antinomianism because the *koinonia* exhibits and engenders a style of life and provides generalizations about the good life which both shape the conscience unconsciously and inform and direct the conscious decisions it makes. The Christian conscience is not without general description although it is not confined by legalistic definition. Thus the community context of the Christian conscience provides content, consensus, and continuity, but by its very nature, love, which is the covenant bond of the Christian conscience, defies complete definition. Its expressions are infinite, and in its freedom, it is sensitive and creative in discerning the appropriate response in the situation.

Responsibility is not a cure-all concept for healing the diseases which plague attempts to aid the recovery of *conscience*. Like conscience, it is, in itself, a neutral term until it is loaded by the commitments of the self who is responding and held responsible. The issue is: to whom or to what and for whom or what is one ultimately responsible? The value of *responsibility* for an understanding of *conscience* is, for this writer, in its social connotations. One thinks of being responsible to and for persons more than to or for abstract principles. Like Christian conscience, Christian responsibility is defined by the covenant bond which lies at the heart. God's love, which both enables and elicits response, defines responsibility as universal, unconditional, concrete, and cooperative with his ongoing creation, judgment, and redemption. The self is included in this responsibility although it is not its source or its focus. Life in Christ as part of his church brings self-realization and social responsibility together because it changes the image of the self one is interested in becoming. Conscience and community need not be antagonists. They can be joint authors of a common call to responsible selfhood in a responsible fellowship with a universal responsibility.

Notes

1.

1. Saul Bellow, *Herzog* (Greenwich, Conn.: Fawcett World Library, 1965), p. 333.
2. Nathan A. Scott, Jr., "The Broken Center: A Definition of the Crisis of Values in Modern Literature," *Symbolism in Religion and Literature,* ed. Rollo May (New York: George Braziller, 1960), pp. 192–193.
3. Wylie Sypher, *Loss of the Self in Modern Literature and Art* (New York: Random House, 1962).
4. William R. Mueller, "A Man for All Seasons," *Theology Today,* Vol. XXIV, No. 2 (July, 1967), p. 248.
5. Michael Novak, Abraham J. Heschel, Robert McAfee Brown, *Vietnam: Crisis of Conscience* (New York: Association Press, 1967).
6. Charles Curran, "The Problem of Conscience and the Twentieth Century," *Ecumenical Dialogue at Harvard,* eds. Samuel H. Miller and G. Ernest Wright (Cambridge, Mass.: Harvard University Press, 1964), p. 267.
7. Paul L. Lehmann, *Ethics in a Christian Context* (New York: Harper & Row, 1963), pp. 333–336.
8. Curran, *op. cit.* A general source for Curran's critique of both these tendencies or trends is Jacques LeClercq, *Christ and the Modern Conscience,* translated by Ronald Matthews (London: Geoffrey Chapman Ltd., 1962), pp. 7–104.
9. Paul Tillich, "Religious Perspectives," *Morality and Beyond,* ed. Ruth Nanda Anshen (New York: Harper & Row, 1963), Vol. 9, p. 75.
10. Lehmann, *Ethics in a Christian Context,* pp. 339–340.
11. Sypher, *Loss of the Self in Modern Literature and Art,* p. 21.
12. Tillich, *Morality and Beyond,* p. 79.
13. George Herbert Mead, *Mind, Self, and Society,* ed. Charles W. Morris (Chicago: University of Chicago Press, 1934), p. 138.
14. A current reduction of conscience to a feeling or psychological fact with a resulting dismissal of its authority is found in R. M. Hare, *The Language of Morals* (New York: Oxford University Press, 1952), pp. 43, 170. According to his view a person might talk of doing the right thing contrary to conscience. Thus, conscience is an emotional reaction and not a moral evaluation.
15. Martin Heidegger, *Existence and Being,* ed. Werner Brock (Chicago: Henry Regnery Co., 1949), pp. 65–66.
16. Tillich, *Morality and Beyond,* p. 80.
17. Gardner Lindzey and Calvin S. Hall, *Theories of Personality* (New York: John Wiley and Sons, Inc., 1957), p. 65.
18. Karen Horney, *The Collected Works of Karen Horney* (New York: W. W. Norton and Co., 1937), Vol. I, p. 230.
19. Erich Fromm, *Man for Himself* (Greenwich, Conn.: Fawcett Publications, 1965), p. 162.

20. *Ibid.*, p. 163.
21. *Ibid.*, p. 174.
22. Roger Shinn, *Man: The New Humanism* (Philadelphia: Westminster Press, 1968), Vol. VI, pp. 176, 179.
23. Erich Fromm, *You Shall Be As Gods: A Radical Interpretation of The Old Testament and Its Tradition* (New York: Holt, Rinehart and Winston, 1966).
24. Thomas Vernor Smith, *The Ethics of Compromise and the Art of Containment* (Boston: Starr King Press, 1956), p. 54.
25. Rolf Hochhuth, *The Deputy* (New York: Grove Press, Inc., 1964), p. 83.
26. Hannah Arendt, *Eichmann in Jerusalem* (New York: Viking Press, 1963).
27. *Ibid.*, pp. 111–112.
28. *Ibid.*
29. Sigmund Freud, *Major Works* (Chicago: Encyclopedia Britannica, 1952), pp. 831–832.
30. Bernard Wand, "The Constant and Function of Conscience," *Journal of Philosophy*, Vol. LVIII, No. 24 (November 23, 1961), p. 771.
31. Lehmann, *Ethics in a Christian Context*, p. 326.
32. Waldo Beach and H. Richard Niebuhr, *Christian Ethics: Sources of the Living Tradition* (New York: Ronald Press Co., 1955), p. 475.
33. Reinhold Niebuhr, *The Nature and Destiny of Man* (New York: Charles Scribner's Sons, 1949).
34. Reinhold Niebuhr, *The Self and the Dramas of History* (New York: Charles Scribner's Sons, 1955).

2

1. Fredrick Denison Maurice, *Conscience* (London: Macmillan and Co., 1883), p. 174.
2. Helmut Thielicke, *Theological Ethics,* (Philadelphia: Fortress Press, 1966), Vol. 1, p. 298.
3. H. Richard Niebuhr, *Christ and Culture* (New York: Harper & Bros., 1951), pp. 190–191.
4. C. A. Pierce, *Conscience in the New Testament* (London: SCM Press, 1955). The inadequacy of Pierce's position for our purposes is seen in his assertion that for the New Testament the Christian should be free of conscience.
5. Paul L. Lehmann, *Ethics in a Christian Context* (New York: Harper & Row, 1963), p. 355.
6. *Ibid.*, pp. 358–359.
7. Maurice, *Conscience*, p. 174.
8. Karl Barth, *Christ and Adam,* trans. T. A. Smail (Edinburgh: Oliver and Boyd, 1956).
9. Paul Ramsey, *Deeds and Rules in Christian Ethics* (New York: Charles Scribner's Sons, 1967), p. 64.
10. Bernhard Häring, *The Law of Christ: Moral Theology for Priest and Laity*, ed. Edwin G. Kaiser (Westminster, Md.: The Newman Press, 1964), Vol. I, p. 14.
11. John Thomas, "Conscience and a Pluralistic Society: Theological and

Sociological Issues," *Ecumenical Dialogue at Harvard* (Cambridge: Harvard University Press), p. 226.

12. Salvador de Madariaga, *Don Quixote* (London: Oxford University Press, 1961), p. 85.

13. H. Richard Niebuhr, "The Ego-Alter Dialectic and the Conscience," *Journal of Philosophy*, XLII (June 21, 1945), p. 352.

14. Häring, *The Law of Christ*, Vol. I, p. 156.

15. F. W. Boreham, *The Uttermost Star* (New York: Abingdon Press, 1919), p. 142.

16. Gilbert Ryle, "Conscience and Moral Convictions," *Analysis*, Vol. VII (June, 1940), p. 35.

17. Bernard Wand, "The Content and Function of Conscience," *Journal of Philosophy*, Vol. LVIII, No. 24 (November, 1961), p. 770.

18. Mark Twain, *Huckleberry Finn* (New York: Washington Square Press, 1961), p. 118.

19. Häring, *The Law of Christ*, Vol. I, p. 156.

20. Dietrich Bonhoeffer, *Ethics*, ed. Eberhard Bethge (New York: Macmillan Co., 1955), p. 196.

21. Joseph Fletcher, *Situation Ethics* (Philadelphia: The Westminster Press, 1966), p. 54.

22. Leonard Louis Levinson, *The Left Handed Dictionary* (New York: The Crowell-Collier Publishing Co., 1963), p. 50.

23. Reinhold Niebuhr, *The Self and the Dramas of History* (New York: Charles Scribner's Sons, 1955), pp. 9, 10.

24. Gordon Allport, *Becoming* (New Haven: Yale University Press, 1955), pp. 71–72. Peter Bertocci, "A Re-interpretation of Moral Obligation," *Philosophy and Phenomenological Research*, Vol. VI (December, 1945), pp. 270–283.

25. Brian Moore, *The Emperor of Ice-Cream* (New York: Viking Press, 1965), p. 250.

26. Levinson, *The Left Handed Dictionary*, p. 51.

27. James N. Lapsley, "A Psycho-Theological Appraisal of the New Left," *Theology Today*, Vol. XXV, No. 4 (January, 1969), p. 456.

28. Gerhart Piers and Milton B. Singer, *Shame and Guilt: A Psycho-analytic and Cultural Study* (Springfield, Ill.: Charles C. Thomas, 1953), pp. 53–54.

29. Helen Merrill Lynd, *On Shame and the Search for Identity* (New York: Harcourt, Brace and Company, 1958), p. 24.

30. James N. Lapsley, "A Psycho-Theological Appraisal of the New Left," *Theology Today*, Vol. XXV, No. 4 (January, 1969), p. 458.

31. Tillich's chapter on conscience in *Morality and Beyond* is entitled "The Transmoral Conscience."

32. Lehmann, *Ethics in a Christian Context*, p. 316.

33. *Ibid.*, p. 350.

34. Joseph Fletcher, *Situation Ethics*, p. 53.

35. Gerhard Ebeling, "Theological Reflexions on Conscience," *Word and Faith*, trans. James W. Leith (Philadelphia: Fortress Press, 1963), p. 417.

36. Eleanor Humes Haney, "A Study of Conscience as It Is Expressed in Race Relations" (Ph.D. thesis, Yale University, 1965), p. 7.

37. Stuart Hampshire, *Thought and Action* (New York: Viking Press, 1959), pp. 220–221.
38. Bernhard Häring. "The 'Heart' in Scripture and Tradition," *The Law of Christ*, Vol. I, p. 209.
39. *Ibid.*, p. 206.
40. Lehmann, *Ethics in a Christian Context*, pp. 352–353.
41. *Ibid.*, p. 353.
42. *Ibid.*, pp. 353–354.
43. *Ibid.*, p. 362.
44. Martin Luther, *Lectures on Genesis, 1535–45, Werke*, ed. J. K. F. Knaake, G. Kawerau, E. Thiele, and others (Weimar: H. Böhlau, 1883), pp. 44, 550, 29 ff.
45. Martin Luther, *Lectures on the Psalms*, ed. J. K. F. Knaake, G. Kawerau, E. Thiele, and others (Weimar: H. Böhlau, 1883), pp. 3, 593, 28–29.
46. Lehmann, *Ethics in a Christian Context*, p. 363.
47. John Calvin, *The Institutes of the Christian Religion*, trans. Ford Lewis Battles, ed. John T. McNeill (Philadelphia: The Westminster Press, 1960), Ch. 19, Paragraphs 2, 4, 6, and 16.
48. Paul Lehmann, "Integrity of Heart: A Comment upon the Preceding Paper," *Ecumenical Dialogue at Harvard*, eds. Samuel H. Miller and G. Ernest Wright (Cambridge, Mass.: Harvard University Press, 1964), p. 278.
49. Helmut Thielicke, *Theological Ethics* (Philadelphia: Fortress Press, 1966), Vol. 1, pp. 327–328.
50. *Ibid.*, p. 300.
51. *Ibid.*, pp. 311 and 300.
52. David Little, "Seminar IV. Conscience in a Pluralistic Society: Theological and Sociological Issues," *Ecumenical Dialogue at Harvard*, eds. Samuel H. Miller and G. Ernest Wright (Cambridge, Mass.: Harvard University Press, 1964), p. 354.
53. Charles Curran, "The Problem of Conscience and the Twentieth Century," *Ecumenical Dialogue at Harvard*, eds. Samuel H. Miller and G. Ernest Wright (Cambridge, Mass.: Harvard University Press, 1964), p. 264.
54. Paul Ramsey, "The Church and the Magistrate," *Christianity and Crisis*, Vol. 25, No. 11 (June 28, 1965), p. 136.
55. Richard Baxter, *The Practical Works of Richard Baxter (A Christian Directory*, Vol. I; London: Arthur Hall and Co., 1847), Part I, chap. iii.
56. In her Ph.D. dissertation, "The Phenomenology of Conscience," (Harvard, 1937), Erminie Huntress appropriates Heidegger's understanding of conscience as one that stands in opposition to all attempts to exhaust the truth about man in terms of scientific "facts." She cites psychology as a guilty party on this count: "The psychologists assume that our existence is obvious and we can go immediately in our investigations to something else, but since psychology is nearer than most of the sciences to being concerned with person existence, 'explaining' what man is, the preliminary assumption is dangerous" (p. 19).
57. Martin Buber, *Between Man and Man*, trans. Ronald Gregor Smith (New York: The Macmillan Co., 1965), p. 65.

58. *Ibid.*, pp. 69–70.
59. Erik H. Erikson, *Childhood and Society* (New York: W. W. Norton & Company, 1963).
    Erik H. Erikson, *Identity and the Life Cycle* (New York: International University Press, 1959).
    Erik H. Erikson, *Insight and Responsibility* (New York: W. W. Norton & Company, 1964).
60. Herbert McCabe, "The Validity of Absolutes," *Commonweal*, LXXXIII (January 14, 1966), p. 443.
61. Hannah Arendt, *The Human Condition* (Garden City, N.Y.: Doubleday & Co., Inc., 1958), p. 46.
62. *Ibid.*
63. Helmut Thielicke, *The Freedom of the Christian Man*, trans. John W. Doberstein (New York: Harper & Row, Publishers, 1963), p. 46.
64. Bonhoeffer and Lehmann fail to provide us with sufficient analysis of selfhood at least in part because of their fears that anthropological analysis may distort Christological proclamation, because Christ must, they say, precede Adam in Christian considerations; because Niebuhr views Christianity as a species, not a genus, of human moral existence. (H. Richard Niebuhr, *The Responsible Self*, New York: Harper & Row, Publishers, 1963, p. 150.) He stresses the continuity between Christian ethics and other modes of existence without diminishing his emphasis on revelation as transformer of religion and natural morality. He writes in the prologue of *The Responsible Self*, "these are the reflections of a Christian who is seeking to understand the mode of his existence and that of his fellow beings as human agents" (p. 42). Ebeling, like Bultmann and Tillich, operates with a hermeneutical circle or method of correlation, which relates proclamation to the reality of man's ethical situation lest it "beat the air." "Reflection on man has a hermeneutical function for theology as a whole," [Ebeling, "Theology and the Evidentness of the Ethical," *Translating Theology into the Modern Age*, Rudolf Bultmann, et al. (New York: Harper and Row, 1965), pp. 96–120.] and anthropolgy is not, as in Bonhoeffer, solely derived from Christology. Theology and ethics begin both with God's revelation and man's situation.

3

1. William Temple, *Mens Creatrix* (London: Macmillan and Co., 1949), p. 182.
2. James Gustafson, "Christian Ethics and Social Policy," *Faith and Ethics*, ed. Paul Ramsey (New York: Harper and Brothers, 1957), p. 122.
3. Dietrich Bonhoeffer, *Ethics*, trans. Eberhard Bethge (New York: Macmillan Co., 1955), p. 222.
4. H. Richard Niebuhr, *The Responsible Self* (New York: Harper & Row, Publishers, 1963), p. 65.
5. *Ibid.*, p. 71.
6. *Ibid.*
7. *Ibid.*, p. 95.

8. Bernard Malamud, *The Assistant* (New York: The New American Library, 1957), p. 72.
9. Niebuhr, *The Responsible Self*, p. 65.
10. *Ibid.*
11. *Ibid.*, p. 61.
12. *Ibid.*, p. 63.
13. In "The Center of Value," which was referred to in note 5, Niebuhr gives a concise exposition of his relational value theory. In part, he says, "Good . . . must be applied to that which meets the needs, which fits the capacities, which corresponds to the potentialities of an existent being" (p. 103). "[Value] is not a function of being as such but of being in relation to being" (p. 107).
14. Niebuhr, *The Responsible Self*, p. 68.
15. *Ibid.*, p. 126.
16. James Gustafson, "Context versus Principles: A Misplaced Debate in Christian Ethics," *Harvard Theological Review*, Vol. 58, No. 2 (April, 1965), p. 185.
17. H. Richard Niebuhr, "The Ego-Alter Dialectic and the Conscience," *The Journal of Philosophy*, Vol. XLII, No. 13 (June 21, 1945), p. 352.
18. Writing later in *The Responsible Self*, p. 75, Niebuhr praises the rejection by Smith and Hume of the "as if" of the duality in the self as presented by Kant. He also indicates knowledge of current social theories of conscience in Freud and in recent analysts, discussions of the logic of moral language.
19. Niebuhr, "The Ego-Alter Dialectic and the Conscience," p. 352.
20. George Herbert Mead, *Mind, Self, and Society*, ed. Charles W. Morris (Chicago: University of Chicago Press, 1934), p. 138.
21. Martin Buber, *I and Thou*, trans. Ronald Gregor Smith (Second Edition, New York: Charles Scribner's Sons, 1958).
22. Niebuhr, *The Responsible Self*, pp. 72–73.
23. H. Richard Niebuhr, *Christ and Culture* (New York: Harper & Brothers, Publishers, 1951), pp. 245–246.
24. Niebuhr, "The Ego-Alter Dialectic and the Conscience," p. 354.
25. George Herbert Mead, *The Philosophy of the Present* (Chicago: Open Court Publishing Co., 1932), p. 190.
26. Niebuhr, "The Ego-Alter Dialectic and the Conscience," p. 354.
27. *Ibid.*
28. *Ibid.*
29. Niebuhr, *The Responsible Self*, p. 77.
30. *Ibid.*
31. *Ibid.*, p. 78.
32. *Ibid.*
33. *Ibid.*, pp. 78–79.
34. Niebuhr, "The Ego-Alter Dialectic and the Conscience," p. 355.
35. Julian Hartt, "The Situation of the Believer," *Faith and Ethics*, ed. Paul Ramsey (New York: Harper and Brothers, 1957), p. 226.
36. *Ibid.*, p. 243.
37. James M. Robinson and John B. Cobb, Jr. (eds.), *The New Hermeneutic* (*New Frontiers in Theology*, Vol. II; New York: Harper & Row, 1964).

38. James M. Robinson, "Hermeneutic Since Barth," in *ibid.*, pp. 47, 48.
39. Gerhard Ebeling, "Reflexions on the Doctrine of the Law," *Word and Faith*, trans. Jas. W. Leith (Philadelphia: Fortress Press, 1963), pp. 277–278.
40. *Ibid.*, p. 410.
41. *Ibid.*, p. 411.
42. *Ibid.*, p. 412.
43. *Ibid.*
44. *Ibid.*
45. *Ibid.*, p. 414.
46. *Ibid.*, p. 416.
47. *Ibid.*, p. 417.
48. *Ibid.*, p. 418.
49. *Ibid.*, p. 419.
50. *Ibid.*, p. 420.
51. *Ibid.*
52. Gerhard Ebeling, "Theology and the Evidentness of the Ethical," *Translating Theology into the Modern Age*, trans. Jas. W. Leith (New York: Harper and Row, 1965), p. 105.
53. *Ibid.*, p. 106.
54. *Ibid.*, p. 108.
55. *Ibid.*, p. 109.
56. *Ibid.*
57. Martin Buber, *Between Man and Man*, trans. Ronald Gregor Smith (New York: The Macmillan Co., 1965), p. 17.
58. Ebeling, "Theology and the Evidentness of the Ethical," p. 112.
59. *Ibid.*, p. 113.
60. *Ibid.*, p. 115.
61. *Ibid.*, p. 117.
62. *Ibid.*
63. *Ibid.*, p. 118.
64. *Ibid.*
65. *Ibid.*
66. *Ibid.*, p. 129.
67. Niebuhr, *The Responsible Self*, pp. 63–64.
68. Ebeling, "Theology and the Evidentness of the Ethical," p. 121.
69. *Ibid.*
70. *Ibid.*
71. *Ibid.*, p. 123.
72. Paul Tillich, *Morality and Beyond* (New York: Harper & Row, Publishers, 1963), Vol. 9, p. 66.
73. Carl Michalson, *Faith for Personal Crises* (New York: Charles Scribner's Sons, 1958), p. 60.
74. Tillich, *Morality and Beyond*, p. 34.
75. Niebuhr, *The Responsible Self*, p. 71.
76. Gordon Allport, *Becoming* (New Haven, Conn.: Yale University Press, 1955), pp. 72–73.
77. Erich Fromm, *Man for Himself* (Greenwich, Conn.: Fawcett Publications, 1965), p. 162.

78. *Ibid.*

79. Emil Brunner, *The Divine Imperative,* trans. Olive Wyon (Philadelphia: The Westminster Press, 1947), p. 156.

80. H. Richard Niebuhr, "The Center of Values" and "Faith in Gods and in God," *Radical Monotheism and Western Culture* (New York: Harper and Brothers, 1960), pp. 100–126.

81. Robert Penn Warren, *The Cave* (New York: Random House, 1959), p. 101.

82. Daniel Callahan, "Self-Identity in an Urban Society," *Theology Today,* Vol. XXIV, No. 1 (April, 1967), p. 31.

83. Erik Erikson, "The Problem of Ego Identity," *Journal of the American Psychoanalytic Association,* IV (1956). Reprinted in *Identity and Anxiety,* eds. Maurice R. Stein, Arthur J. Vidich, and David Manning White (New York: The Free Press of Glencoe, 1963), p. 38.

84. Robert Lee, "Delinquent Youth in a Normless Time," *Christian Century,* Vol. LXXIX (December 5, 1962), p. 1477.

85. John L. Thomas, "Conscience and a Pluralistic Society: Theological and Sociological Issues," *Ecumenical Dialogue at Harvard,* eds. Samuel M. Miller and G. Ernest Wright (Cambridge, Mass.: Harvard University Press, 1964), p. 215.

86. Robert Bolt, *A Man for All Seasons* (New York: Random House, 1962), p. xi.

87. Wylie Sypher, *Loss of the Self in Modern Literature and Art* (New York: Random House, 1962).

88. Daniel Callahan, "Self-Identity in an Urban Society," p. 38.

89. Gabriel Vahanian, *The Death of God,* ed. George Braziller (New York: George Braziller, 1961), pp. 182–183.

90. John R. Fry, *The Immobilized Christian: A Study of His Pre-ethical Situation* (Philadelphia: The Westminster Press, 1963), p. 119.

91. Rollo May, "The Significance of Symbols," *Symbolism in Religion and Literature,* ed. Rollo May (New York: George Braziller, 1960), p. 34.

92. *Ibid.,* p. 33.

93. Reinhold Niebuhr, *The Self and the Dramas of History* (New York: Charles Scribner's Sons, 1955), pp. 234–235.

94. *Ibid.,* pp. 229–230.

95. Roger L. Shinn, *Man: The New Humanism* (Philadelphia: The Westminster Press, 1968), Vol. VI, p. 179.

96. *Ibid.,* p. 180.

97. Dietrich Bonhoeffer, *Ethics* (New York: The Macmillan Co., 1955), p. 215.

98. Emil Brunner, *The Divine Imperative,* p. 157.

99. Peter Bertocci and Richard Millard, *Personality and the Good* (New York: David McKay Company, Inc., 1963) pp. 455-456, 457. Where critical conscience clashes with automatic or traditional conscience, a change in the values of conscience takes place or is in the process of doing so. R. M. Ware in his *The Language of Morals* (New York: Oxford University Press, 1952) takes a different, and, this writer contends, untenable position. He reduces statements about conscience to statements of psychological fact. Conscience is only a feeling, and it is possible for one to speak of acting on his convictions as to the right thing to do contrary to the

pangs of conscience (pp. 43, 170). Conscience as fact or feeling is thus separated from moral obligation or valuation. We are objecting, with Martin C. McGuire in his article "On Conscience," *Journal of Philosophy*, Vol. LX, No. 10 (May 9, 1963), pp. 262–263, that what one believes to be right and what conscience tells him will ultimately coincide if it is truly the voice of conscience speaking. Where the two disagree, a conversion of conscience is taking place through critical reappraisal of the sanctions of automatic conscience.

100. Hyphenated since a word is a deed and a deed is a word.

101. After the view of conscience developed here had been worked out in the writer's dissertation, the published abstract of Dr. Eleanor Humes Haney's dissertation came to his attention. In the abstract and later in the dissertation itself, which Dr. Haney graciously loaned to me, I found that in Dr. Haney's first chapter she had presented conscience in a way very similar to what I was attempting before proceeding to test her definition using numerous case studies of people who had figured in racial crisis and civil rights and supported integration in various ways. Since Dr. Haney and I both studied under H. Richard Niebuhr and James Gustafson at Yale and have both been deeply influenced by their thought, it is not surprising that there should be similarity in our approaches, while our dissertations were quite different in type, focus, and coverage. I must compliment Dr. Haney on a brilliant dissertation and thank her for helping me to understand better what I was trying to say in mine. After surveying the literature which related to conscience either by name or otherwise, Dr. Haney observes the four interpretations of conscience, which occur over and over: "These are the activity of moral judgment in response to particular events and demands, the authority for judgment, the integrity of the self and its consistency of judgment and action, and a particular body of conviction to which the self is committed." Dr. Haney gives her definition as follows: "The concept conscience may be said to refer to self's patterning of its life in relation to the demands of its moral situations, to others whose approval it cherishes and authority it respects, to a movement toward personal integrity or wholeness, and to the convictions about the world that interpret and inform action" (p. 6). I find nothing to criticize in this definition. I only wish I had written it myself, and I believe that my definition was clarified through my reading of her work although it is based on the understanding that I had worked out before I had access to her efforts.

4

1. Martin Luther, *Here I Stand* (New York: The New American Library of World Literature, 1950), p. 144.

2. Robert Bolt, *A Man for All Seasons* (New York: Random House, 1962), pp. xv-xvi.

3. Ira Glasser, "The Trial of Captain Howard Levy," *Christianity and Crisis*, Vol. XXVII (August 7, 1967), pp. 193–194.

4. Waldo Beach, "The Meaning and Authority of Conscience in Protestant Thought of Seventeenth Century England," (Ph.D. thesis, Yale University, 1944).

5. Christopher Jencks, "Limits of the New Left," *The New Republic*, Vol. 157, No. 17 (October 21, 1967), p. 19.

6. Helmut Thielicke, *Theological Ethics* (Philadelphia: Fortress Press, 1966), Vol. 1, p. 13.

7. André Gide, *The Immoralist* (New York: Alfred A. Knopf, 1966), p. 11.

8. Albert Camus, *The Fall* (New York: Alfred A. Knopf, 1958), p. 133.

9. Paul Hessert, "Christian Life," *New Directions in Theology Today* (Philadelphia: Westminster Press, 1967), Vol. V, p. 92.

10. Marcus Raskin, (Lecture) "Being and Doing: Decolonization and Reconstruction in American Life" (East Lansing, Mich.: Michigan State University, June, 1967).

11. Walter Lippmann, "The University," *The New Republic* (May 28, 1966), p. 17.

12. *Ibid.*

13. *Ibid.*

14. Harvey Wheeler, "The Civilization of the Dialogue," *Dialogue on Education*, eds. Robert Theobald and Richard Kean (Indianapolis: Bobbs-Merrill, Inc., 1967), p. 108.

15. John McHale, "Education for Real," *Dialogue on Education*, eds. Robert Theobald and Richard Kean (Indianapolis: Bobbs-Merrill, Inc., 1967), p. 122.

16. "Semester of Discontent," National Education Television Production.

17. Edward A. Tiryakian, "A Perspective on the Relationship of Student and University," *Duke Alumni Bulletin* (August, 1967), p. 22.

18. Kenneth Boulding, *The Image* (Ann Arbor, Mich.: University of Michigan Press, 1956), p. 103.

19. *Ibid.*

20. H. D. Wendland, "The Theology of the Responsible Self," *Christian Social Ethics in a Changing World*, ed. John C. Bennett (New York: Association Press, 1966), pp. 139–140.

21. Christopher Jencks, "The Limits of the New Left," *The New Republic*, Vol. 157, No. 17 (October 21, 1967), pp. 20–21.

22. H. Richard Niebuhr, "The Ego-Alter Dialectic and the Conscience," *Journal of Philosophy*, Vol. XLII, No. 13 (June 21, 1945), p. 356.

23. *Ibid.*

24. *Ibid.*

25. *Ibid.*

26. *Ibid.* Pfeutze, in *The Social Self*, points out that both Mead and Freud neglect the factors of uniqueness and autonomy in the self. They surrender the private. At least one of the reasons for this lack and the deficiencies of Mead's "generalized other" is the absence of a universal other or God (pp. 336–339).

27. Boulding, *The Image*, p. 74.

28. Niebuhr, "The Ego-Alter Dialectic and the Conscience," pp. 356–357.

29. Emil Brunner, *The Christian Doctrine of the Church, Faith and the Consummation* (Dogmatics Vol. III) (London: Lutterworth Press, 1962), pp. 19–37.

30. Niebuhr, "The Ego-Alter Dialectic and the Conscience," p. 357.

31. *Ibid.*

32. Josiah Royce, *The Philosophy of Loyalty* (New York: The Macmillan Co., 1920).
33. H. Richard Niebuhr, *The Responsible Self* (New York: Harper and Brothers, 1963), p. 83.
34. Fuller elaboration of this theme is found in Niebuhr's *Radical Monotheism and Western Culture* in numerous passages.
35. Niebuhr, *The Responsible Self*, p. 85.
36. Eleanor Humes Haney, "A Study of Conscience as It Is Expressed in Race Relations," p. 36 f. Dr. Haney cites James Nelson in asking whether all communities transcend themselves and indicates that such self-transcendence is not necessarily true of a family.
37. Reinhold Niebuhr, *Man's Nature and His Communities* (New York: Charles Scribner's Sons, 1965), p. 31.
38. *Ibid.*, p. 32.
39. F. W. Dillistone, "Crisis of Authority," *Theology Today*, Vol. XXIV, No. 2 (July, 1967). Dillistone enters a caveat, against linking words, persons, and institutions quite so easily. "Words are more flexible than institutions; persons are more flexible than words. Institutions are *least* able to be *vehicles*." His point is well worth making but community authority cannot be legitimately made a third-class citizen, and there is a sense in which an organized community is an institution (p. 129).
40. Paul Lehmann, *Ethics in a Christian Context* (New York: Harper and Row, 1963), p. 316.
41. Dietrich Bonhoeffer, *Sanctorum Communio* (London: William Collins Sons & Company, 1963), p. 184.
42. James Gustafson, "Introduction," *The Responsible Self*, pp. 22–23.
43. Bernhard Häring, *The Law of Christ: Moral Theology for Priest and Laity*, trans. Edwin G. Kaiser (Westminster, Md.: The Newman Press, 1964), Vol. I, p. 229.
44. *Ibid.*, Vol. I, p. 150.
45. James Gustafson, "Theology and Ethics," *The Scope of Theology*, ed. Daniel T. Jenkins (Cleveland: The World Publishing Company, 1965), p. 132.
46. Dietrich Bonhoeffer, *Ethics*, trans. Eberhard Bethge (New York: Macmillan Co., 1955), p. 213.
47. Reinhold Niebuhr, *Man's Nature and His Communities*, p. 18.
48. Niebuhr, "The Ego-Alter Dialectic and the Conscience," p. 358.
49. Niebuhr, *The Responsible Self*, p. 88.
50. *Ibid.*, p. 87.
51. *Ibid.*
52. *Ibid.*, pp. 87–88.
53. Reinhold Niebuhr, *Man's Nature and His Communities*, p. 75.
54. Martin Buber, *Between Man and Man*, trans. Ronald Gregor Smith (New York: The Macmillan Co., 1955), pp. 32–33.
55. *Ibid.*, p. 31.

5

1. Dietrich Bonhoeffer, *Ethics* (New York: The Macmillan Co., 1955), pp. 212–213. Italics added.

2. Reinhold Niebuhr, *Man's Nature and His Communities* (New York: Charles Scribner's Sons, 1965), pp. 107–108.
3. *Ibid.*, p. 119.
4. Lester A. Kirkendall, "An Emerging Morality And The College Counselor," *motive*, Vol. XXVIII, No. 7 (April, 1968), p. 33.
5. *Ibid.*, p. 33.
6. Bonhoeffer, *Ethics*, p. 145. Cf. Karl Barth, *The Epistle to the Romans*, trans. Edwyn C. Hoskyns (London: Oxford University Press, 1933), pp. 490–491, 148.
7. Helmut Thielicke, *Theological Ethics* (Philadelphia: Fortress Press, 1966), pp. 282, 309.
8. Paul Lehmann, *Ethics in a Christian Context* (New York: Harper and Row, 1963), p. 80.
9. Bernard Malamud, *The Assistant* (New York: The New American Library, 1957), pp. 137–138.
10. Bonhoeffer, *Ethics*, p. 145.
11. T. S. Eliot, *The Cocktail Party* (New York: Harcourt, Brace and Company, 1950), pp. 136–137.
12. Luigi Pirandello, *Six Characters in Search of an Author*, Act I. *Naked Masks*, ed. Eric Bentley (New York: E. P. Dutton and Co., 1950), pp. 231–232.
13. H. Richard Niebuhr, "The Ego-Alter Dialectic and the Conscience," *Journal of Philosophy*, XLII, No. 13 (June 21, 1945), p. 359.
14. Bernhard Häring, *The Law of Christ*, trans. Edwin G. Kaiser (Westminster, Md.: The Newman Press, 1965), Vol. I, p. 136.
15. Helmut Thielicke, *Theological Ethics*, p. 142.
16. *Ibid.*, pp. 323–324.
17. *Ibid.*, pp. 311, 300.
18. Leslie Dewart, *The Future of Belief: Theism in a World Come of Age* (New York: Herder and Herder, 1966), pp. 81 f, 174 ff.
19. H. Richard Niebuhr, *The Responsible Self* (New York: Harper and Brothers, 1963), p. 143.
20. *Ibid.*, pp. 154–155.
21. *Ibid.*, p. 163.
22. *Ibid.*, p. 177.
23. *Ibid.*, pp. 177–178.
24. H. Richard Niebuhr, "The Ego-Alter Dialectic and the Conscience," p. 359.

6

1. Daniel Callahan, "Self-Identity in an Urban Society," *Theology Today*, Vol. XXIV, No. 1 (April, 1967), pp. 37, 38, 39.
2. H. Richard Niebuhr, *The Responsible Self* (New York: Harper & Row, Publishers, 1963), pp. 144–145.
3. James Gustafson, "Christian Faith and Moral Action," *Christian Century*, Vol. LXXXII (November 3, 1965), p. 1347.
4. Helmut Thielicke, *Theological Ethics* (Philadelphia: Fortress Press, 1966), p. 193.
5. *Ibid.*

6. Bernhard Häring, *The Law of Christ: Moral Theology for Priest and Laity*, trans. Edwin G. Kaiser (Westminster, Md.: The Newman Press, 1964), Vol. I, p. 133.
7. Sallie McFague TeSelle, *Literature and the Christian Life* (New Haven: Yale University Press, 1966), p. 26.
8. *Ibid.*, p. 27.
9. Eduard Schweizer, *Lordship and Discipleship* (London: SCM Press, 1960), p. 126 ff.
10. *Ibid.*, p. 12.
11. *Ibid.*, p. 128.
12. C. H. Dodd, *Gospel and Law* (New York: Columbia University Press, 1951), p. 71.
13. Amos N. Wilder, "The Cross: Social Trauma or Redemption," *Symbolism in Religion and Literature,* ed. Rollo May (New York: George Braziller, Inc., 1960), p. 101.
14. Michael Harrington, "Christ as a Hipster," *Cavalier* Magazine (March, 1967).
15. Wilder, "The Cross: Social Trauma or Redemption," p. 100.
16. Callahan, "Self-Identity in an Urban Society," p. 38.
17. *Ibid.*
18. Thielicke, *Theological Ethics,* pp. 192, 193, 194.
19. Dietrich Bonhoeffer, *Ethics,* ed. Eberhard Bethge (New York: Macmillan Co., 1955), p. 18.
20. *Ibid.*, p. 19.
21. *Ibid.*, p. 24.
22. *Ibid.*, p. 25.
23. *Ibid.*, p. 194.
24. *Ibid.*, p. 195.
25. *Ibid.*, pp. 210, 213.
26. Häring, *The Law of Christ*, Vol. I, p. 52.
27. Bonhoeffer, *Ethics*, pp. 198–199.
28. *Ibid.*, pp. 200, 201.
29. J. H. Burtness and J. P. Kildahl (eds.), *The New Community in Christ* (Minneapolis, Minn.: Augsburg Publishing House, 1963), pp. 89 ff.
30. Callahan, "Self-Identity in an Urban Society," p. 42.
31. Bonhoeffer, *Ethics,* p. 20.
32. *Ibid.*, p. 22.
33. Paul L. Lehmann, *Ethics in a Christian Context* (New York: Harper and Row, 1963), p. 49. This statement could easily have been made by Bonhoeffer.
34. *Ibid.*, p. 63.
35. *Ibid.*, p. 55.
36. James Gustafson, "Context versus Principles: A Misplaced Debate in Christian Ethics," *Harvard Theological Review,* Vol. LVIII (April, 1965), p. 181.
37. *Ibid.*
38. Lehmann, *Ethics in a Christian Context,* p. 131.
39. *Ibid.*, pp. 76–77.
40. *Ibid.*, p. 316.

41. *Ibid.*, p. 288.
42. James Gustafson, "Christian Faith and Moral Action," p. 1346.
43. Niebuhr, *The Responsible Self*, p. 65.
44. William Lee Miller, *The Protestant and Politics* (Philadelphia: Westminster Press, 1958), p. 58.
45. John W. Gardner, *Self-Renewal* (New York: Harper & Row, Publishers, 1964), p. 124.
46. Niebuhr, *The Responsible Self*, pp. 63–64.
47. Daisuke Kitagawa, "The Person and Community," *Revolution and Renewal* (July 1, 1965), pp. 35, 36.
48. Callahan, "Self-Identity in an Urban Society," pp. 36–37.
49. Walter Lippmann, "The University," *The New Republic* (May 28, 1966), pp. 17–19.
50. *Ibid.*, p. 20.
51. *Ibid.*
52. Thomas Langford, "Campus Turmoil: A Religious Dimension," *Christian Century*, Vol. LXXXIV, No. 6 (February 8, 1967).
53. *Ibid.*, p. 173.
54. Paul Goodman, "Student Chaplain," *The New Republic* (January 7, 1967), p. 29.
55. Langford, "Campus Turmoil: A Religious Dimension," p. 174.
56. Goodman, "Student Chaplain," p. 31.
57. Harvey Cox, "Revolt in the Church," *Playboy.*
58. *Ibid.*, p. 140.
59. *Ibid.*
60. Callahan, "Self-Identity in an Urban Society," p. 37.
61. Emil Brunner, *The Misunderstanding of the Church* (London: Lutterworth Press, 1952), p. 29.
62. Harvey Cox, *Secular City* (New York: The Macmillan Co., 1965).
63. Samuel S. Hill, Jr., "How Worldly Should Be the Church?" *New Wine*, Vol. V, No. 2 (Winter, 1967), p. 20.
64. James Gustafson, "A Theology of Christian Community?" *Man in Community*, ed. Egbert de Vries (New York: Association Press, 1966), p. 176.
65. *Ibid.*
66. George Bernard Shaw, *Misalliance, The Dark Lady of the Sonnets and Fanny's First Play* (London: Constable and Co., 1914), pp. 58, 59.
67. John Bennett, "The Church and the Secular," *Christianity and Crisis*, Vol. XXVI, No. 22 (December 26, 1966), p. 296.
68. Michael Novak, "Christianity: Renewed or Slowly Abandoned?" *Daedalus*, Vol. 96, No. 1 (Winter, 1967), p. 262.
69. Gustafson, "A Theology of Christian Community?" p. 177.
70. Michael Harrington, "Christ as a Hipster."
71. Eleanor Humes Haney, "A Study of Conscience as It Is Expressed in Race Relations" (Ph.D. thesis, Yale University, 1965), pp. 335, 336.
72. *Ibid.*, p. 330.

7

1. George Bernard Shaw, *Misalliance, The Dark Lady of the Sonnets and Fanny's First Play* (London: Constable and Co., 1914), p. 33.

2. Dietrich Bonhoeffer, *Ethics*, trans. Eberhard Bethge (New York: Macmillan Co., 1955), pp. 220–221.

3. H. Richard Niebuhr, *The Purpose of the Church and Its Ministry* (New York: Harper and Row, 1956), pp. 35, 36.

4. James Gustafson, "Context versus Principles: A Misplaced Debate in Christian Ethics," *Harvard Theological Review*, Vol. LVIII (April, 1965).

5. *Ibid.*, p. 192.

6. James Gustafson, "How Does Love Reign?" *Christian Century*, Vol. LXXXIII, No. 20 (May 18, 1966), p. 654.

7. Bonhoeffer, *Ethics*, p. 77.

8. *Ibid.*, p. 31.

9. *Ibid.*, p. 23.

10. *Ibid.*, p. 161.

11. *Ibid.*

12. *Ibid.*, p. 163.

13. *Ibid.*, p. 328.

14. James Gustafson, "Theology and Ethics," *The Scope of Theology*, ed. Daniel T. Jenkins (Cleveland: The World Publishing Co., 1965), p. 131 f.

15. Gerhard Ebeling, "Theology and the Evidentness of the Ethical," *Translating Theology into the Modern Age*, trans. Jas. W. Leith, Rudolf Bultmann *et al.* (New York: Harper and Row, 1965), p. 108. Ebeling's version of commandment as the demand of the given is likewise an attempt to achieve concreteness in place of the abstractness in which the given of the ethical values precedes the demand of the given which confronts the self in the situation.

16. Bonhoeffer, *Ethics*, pp. 250, 233.

17. *Ibid.*, p. 248.

18. *Ibid.*, p. 164.

19. *Ibid.*, p. 203.

20. *Ibid.*, p. 204.

21. *Ibid.*, p. 203.

22. *Ibid.*, p. 204.

23. *Ibid.*, p. 207.

24. *Ibid.*, p. 201.

25. Paul Lehmann, *Ethics in a Christian Context* (New York: Harper and Row, 1963), p. 45.

26. *Ibid.*, pp. 148 ff, 152.

27. Lehmann, *Ethics in a Christian Context*, p. 350.

28. *Ibid.*, pp. 124–133.

29. Helmut Thielicke, *Theological Ethics* (Philadelphia: Fortress Press, 1966), Vol. 1, p. 650.

30. *Ibid.*, p. 651.

31. *Ibid.*, p. 652.

32. *Ibid.*

33. *Ibid.*, p. 653.

34. Eleanor Humes Haney, "A Study of Conscience as It Is Expressed in Race Relations" (Ph.D. thesis, Yale University, 1965), pp. 15 ff.

35. Joseph Fletcher, *Situation Ethics* (Philadelphia: The Westminster Press, 1966), p. 53.

36. Gustafson, "How Does Love Reign?" p. 654.
37. Lester A. Kirkendall, "An Emerging Morality And The College Counselor," *motive*, Vol. XXVIII, No. 7 (April, 1968), p. 32.
38. John Calvin, *Institutes of the Christian Religion*, Book II, Chapter 7.
39. James Gustafson, "Christian Faith and Moral Action," *Christian Century*, Vol. LXXXII (November 3, 1965), p. 1346.
40. Joseph Fletcher, "Anglican Theology and the Ethics of Natural Law," *Christian Social Ethics in a Changing World*, ed. John C. Bennett (New York: Association Press, 1966), p. 328.
41. Gustafson, "Theology and Ethics," p. 654.
42. Joseph Fletcher, *Moral Responsibility* (Philadelphia: Westminster Press), pp. 236–237.
43. Bonhoeffer, *Ethics*, p. 229.
44. James Gustafson, "A Theology of Christian Community?," *Man in Community*, ed. Egbert de Vries (New York: Association Press, 1966), p. 188, Note 5.
45. Gustafson, "A Theology of Christian Community?," p. 188.
46. *Ibid.*, p. 186.
47. *Ibid.*, p. 187.
48. Paul Hessert, *Christian Life* (Philadelphia: Westminster Press, 1967), pp. 156–157.
49. Bonhoeffer, *Ethics*, p. 201.
50. *Ibid.*, p. 229.
51. *Ibid.*, pp. 216–217.
52. By contrast, Joseph Fletcher is one of numerous contextualists who insist that "love is always good." *Situation Ethics* (Philadelphia: Westminster Press, 1966), chs. III, IV.
53. Bernhard Häring, *The Law of Christ: Moral Theology for Priest and Laity*, trans. Edwin G. Kaiser (Westminster, Md.: The Newman Press, 1964), Vol. I, p. 247.
54. *Ibid.*, pp. 44–45.
55. See Thielicke's assertion that the law is not for us to the extent we are just. Vol. 1, p. 130.
56. Häring, *The Law of Christ*, Vol. I, p. 264.
57. *Ibid.*, Vol. I, p. 296.
58. *Ibid.*, Vol. I, p. 306.
59. Psalms 19 and 119.
60. Bonhoeffer, *Ethics*, pp. 326–327.
61. Lehmann, *Ethics in a Christian Context*, pp. 129–130.
62. Häring, *The Law of Christ*, Vol. I, p. 288.
63. Helmut Thielicke, *Theological Ethics*, Vol. 1.
64. See previously cited article by Gustafson, "Context versus Principles: A Misplaced Debate in Christian Ethics."
65. Sallie McFague TeSelle, *Literature and the Christian Life* (New Haven: Yale University Press, 1966), pp. 146–152.
66. *Ibid.*, p. 152.
67. Franklin Sherman, "Act and Being," *The Place of Bonhoeffer*, edited by Martin E. Marty (New York: Association Press, 1962), p. 105. Sherman is speaking about an increasing appreciation in the later Barth for this

constance and continuity which defies the reduction of ethics to a "mere series of discrete acts and situations." However, no distortion is involved in using this development to back up Bonhoeffer's position. Sherman does the same.

68. Rolf Hochhuth, *The Deputy*, trans. Richard and Clara Winston (New York: Grove Press, 1964), p. 83.
69. Reinhold Niebuhr, *The Nature and Destiny of Man* (New York: Charles Scribner's Sons, 1955), p. 226.
70. *Ibid.*, pp. 220–221.
71. Thomas Vernor Smith, *The Ethics of Compromise and the Art of Containment* (Boston: Starr King Press, 1956), p. 54.
72. Gustafson, "Theology and Ethics," p. 129.
73. Bonhoeffer, *Ethics*, p. 216.
74. Daniel Callahan, "Cosmic Purpose and Self-Identity," *Theology Today*, Vol. XXV (July, 1968), pp. 169–184.
75. Michael Novak, "Secular Style and Natural Law," *Christianity and Crisis*, Vol. XXVI (July 26, 1966), p. 166.
76. *Ibid.*
77. *Ibid.*
78. Gustafson, "Theology and Ethics," p. 129.
79. Michael Novak, "The Christian and the Atheist," *Christianity and Crisis*, Vol. XXVI (March 21, 1966), p. 55.
80. *Ibid.*
81. *Ibid.*
82. H. Richard Niebuhr, *The Meaning of Revelation* (New York: The Macmillan Co., 1941), pp. 163–164.
83. *Ibid.*, pp. 165–166.
84. *Ibid.*, pp. 166–167.
85. Bonhoeffer, *Ethics*, pp. 225–226.
86. Niebuhr, *The Meaning of Revelation*, pp. 170–171.
87. *Ibid.*, p. 171.
88. Paul Tillich, *Morality and Beyond* (New York: Harper & Row, Publishers, 1963), p. 42.
89. Thielicke, *Theological Ethics.* Vol. 1, p. 645.
90. *Ibid.*, p. 646.
91. *Ibid.*, pp. 646–647.
92. Harry R. Davis and Robert C. Good (eds.), *Reinhold Niebuhr on Politics* (New York: Charles Scribner's Sons, 1960), p. 147.
93. Gabriel Fackre, "Ethical Guidelines for the Control of Life," *Christianity and Crisis*, Vol. XXIX, No. 5 (March 31, 1969), p. 70.